THE COCKTAIL

the cocktail

200 FABULOUS DRINKS

JANE ROCCA

Drawings by Kat Macleod

JEREMY P. TARCHER/PENGUIN
a member of
Penguin Group (USA) Inc.
New York

JEREMY P. TARCHER/PENGUIN
Published by the Penguin Group
Penguin Group (USA) Inc., 375 Hudson Street, New York, New York 10014, USA
Penguin Group (Canada), 90 Eglinton Avenue East, Suite 700, Toronto, Ontario M4P 2Y3, Canada
(a division of Pearson Penguin Canada Inc.)
Penguin Books Ltd, 80 Strand, London WC2R 0RL, England
Penguin Ireland, 25 St Stephen's Green, Dublin 2, Ireland (a division of Penguin Books Ltd)
Penguin Group (Australia), 250 Camberwell Road, Camberwell, Victoria 3124, Australia
(a division of Pearson Australia Group Pty Ltd)
Penguin Books India Pvt Ltd, 11 Community Centre, Panchsheel Park, New Delhi—110 017, India
Penguin Group (NZ), Cnr Airborne and Rosedale Roads, Albany, Auckland 1310, New Zealand
(a division of Pearson New Zealand Ltd)
Penguin Books (South Africa) (Pty) Ltd, 24 Sturdee Avenue, Rosebank, Johannesburg 2196, South Africa

Penguin Books Ltd, Registered Offices: 80 Strand, London WC2R 0RL, England

Previously published in Australia by Hardie Grant Books
www.hardiegrant.com.au
First Jeremy P. Tarcher edition 2006
Text copyright © 2005 by Jane Rocca
Illustrations © 2005 by Kat Macleod

Most Tarcher/Penguin books are available at special quantity discounts for bulk purchase for sales promotions,
premiums, fund-raising, and educational needs. Special books or book excerpts also can be created to fit specific
needs. For details, write Penguin Group (USA) Inc. Special Markets, 375 Hudson Street, New York, NY 10014.

An application to register this book for cataloging has been submitted to the Library of Congress.
ISBN 1-58542-536-2

Printed in China
1 3 5 7 9 10 8 6 4 2

Text design by Simone Elder
Index by Fay Donlevy

The recipes contained in this book are to be followed exactly as written. The publisher is not
responsible for your specific health or allergy needs that may require medical supervision.
The publisher is not responsible for any adverse reactions to the recipes contained in this book.

While the author has made every effort to provide accurate telephone numbers and Internet addresses at the
time of publication, neither the publisher nor the author assumes any responsibility for errors, or for changes
that occur after publication. Further, the publisher does not have any control over and does not assume any
responsibility for author or third-party websites or their content.

CONTENTS

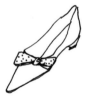
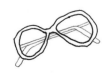

GLASS TYPES

Martini glass

This glass has a triangle-bowl design with a long stem, and is used for a wide range of straight-up (without ice) cocktails, including martinis, manhattans, metropolitans and gimlets. It's perfect for strong drinks and strong personalities.

Highball glass

A tall, straight-sided glass used for long drinks. Highball glasses are generally used to serve light spirits.

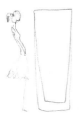

Collins glass

Shaped like a highball glass but taller, the Collins glass was originally used for the line of Collins gin drinks. It's now used for tropical and exotic cocktails.

Tumbler

A glass that traditionally has a rounded bottom and is used to serve dark spirits.

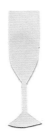

Champagne flute

This is ideal for cocktail drinks whose key ingredients include Champagne or wine.

Pilsner glass

A tall, footed glass generally used to serve beer.

Margarita glass

This slightly larger, rounded approach to a martini glass has a broad rim for holding salt —ideal for margaritas. It's also used for daiquiris.

Shot glass

Usually used for straight booze. It's a small glass, holding about 1 ounce.

Old-fashioned glass

Also known as the rocks glass, this is a short, round glass suitable for drinks served on the rocks. It's for the serious drinker within.

Whiskey sour glass

This glass is stemmed, with a wide opening. It's a small version of a Champagne flute.

Liqueur glass

A small, stemmed glass for serving rich liqueurs.

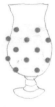

Hurricane glass

A tall and elegant glass named for its resemblance to a hurricane lamp. It's mostly used for exotic cocktails.

Goblet

A drinking glass that has a base and stem.

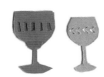

Small wine glass

A small glass used to serve wine or port, usually with engraving around the glass.

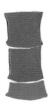

Bamboo glass

A glass designed by May Wong that represents the curvature of a natural bamboo structure.

The Cocktail

NOTES

MUDDLING
In a nutshell, when a recipe requires you to muddle an ingredient, you need a wooden pestle to crush it or break it down. Fruit, herbs and sugar are often muddled to unleash flavor or create a paste.

INFUSING SPIRITS
Many spirits now come in different flavors, but some recipes will require some homemade infusions.

You can flavor the alcohol in two ways:

Infusion/maceration:

Place the ingredients with the alcohol in an airtight container until the flavor is absorbed to your liking (a few days). Store the container at room temperature, out of direct sunlight. You will need to check the infusion every day as after a week the alcohol can take on a stale or bitter flavor, depending on the ingredients.

Pan infusion:

Heat the alcohol in a saucepan with the ingredients until it simmers. Let it sit for up to three hours, then strain alcohol into its original bottle. This method is only suitable for fruit- and sugar-based infusions—not flowers.

champagne chic

❣

There's nothing quite like a glass of bubbly; it's the perfect social lubricant, helping you on your tipsy way as you mingle with friends (and dark strangers). But Champagne conjures romanticism of an old-world kind as well: gorgeous evening gowns and Champagne flutes sparkling at the surface, held aloft by delicate, feminine wrists.

Champagne is dreamlike, forthrightly sophisticated and ever so womanly. It's the ultimate accessory for when you're looking your glammed-up best.

It might be considered the flirty, giddy staple, tottering around on heels, but Champagne also has substance and body. It's the leggy blonde who also boasts a degree in neuroscience. Champagne can be tingly and sweet, fruity or simply brut dry—the flavors taking you on all sorts of journeys—as versatile and varied as those who drink it.

The Bellini is a peachy classic one mustn't pass up, but those hell-bent on the weightiness of beer should opt for the Black Velvet, steeped in creamy, frothy Guinness. However indulged, Champagne is for girls who just want to have fun, for those nights tinged with debauchery and that certain sparkle of life.

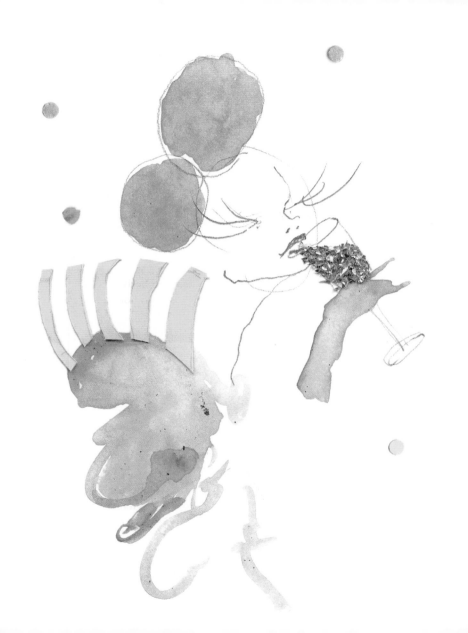

CLASSIC CHAMPAGNE COCKTAIL

Champagne flute

INGREDIENTS

sugar cube
2 dashes of Angostura bitters
3 oz. Champagne
½ oz. cognac
twist of lemon
slice of orange to garnish

METHOD

Soak sugar cube with Angostura
bitters in a Champagne flute.
Add Champagne and cognac,
squeeze in a twist of lemon and
garnish with half a slice of orange.

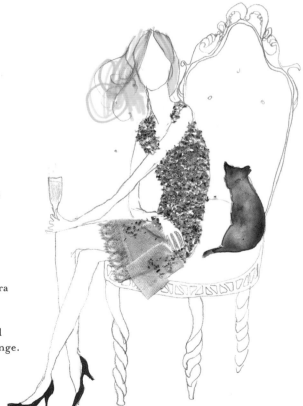

BLACK VELVET

Champagne flute

INGREDIENTS

3 oz. Guinness Stout
3 oz. Champagne

METHOD

Fill half a flute with Guinness. Float an equal part of Champagne on top.

MORNING GLORY

Champagne flute

INGREDIENTS

2½ oz. chilled Champagne
2½ oz. orange juice
1 tbsp. triple sec
orange slice to garnish

METHOD

Fill three-quarters of a flute with Champagne, add orange juice and triple sec, and then garnish with an orange slice.

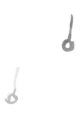
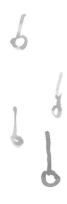

CAROLINA
Wine glass

INGREDIENTS
2 oz. Strega
2 oz. Champagne

METHOD
Pour Strega into a chilled wine glass, add Champagne and stir slightly.

FLIRTINI
Martini glass

INGREDIENTS
2 pieces of fresh pineapple
1 tbsp. Cointreau
1 tbsp. vodka
1 oz. pineapple juice
3 oz. Champagne
cherry to garnish

METHOD
Muddle the pineapple pieces and Cointreau. Add vodka and pineapple juice, then stir. Strain into a chilled martini glass and top with Champagne. Garnish with a cherry and serve.

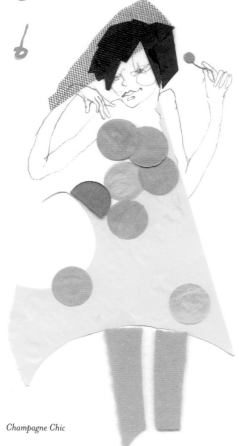

CHERRY CHAMPAGNE
Champagne flute

INGREDIENTS

4 oz. Champagne
1½ oz. cherry brandy

METHOD
Combine ingredients in a
Champagne flute and serve.

FRENCH 75
Collins glass

INGREDIENTS
2 oz. sour mix
1½ oz. cognac
5 oz. Champagne

METHOD
Combine sour mix and cognac in a
Collins glass with a little ice, and stir.
Fill with Champagne, then garnish
with a French flag!

BELLINI
Champagne flute

INGREDIENTS
1 oz. fresh peach puree or nectar
3 oz. Champagne
peach slices to garnish

METHOD
Pour peach puree into a Champagne
flute. Gently top with Champagne and
garnish with a fresh peach slice.

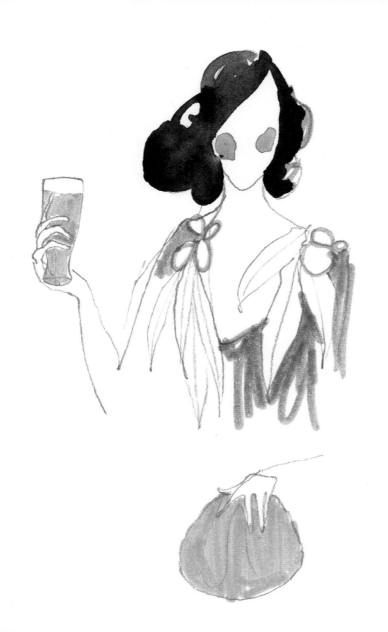

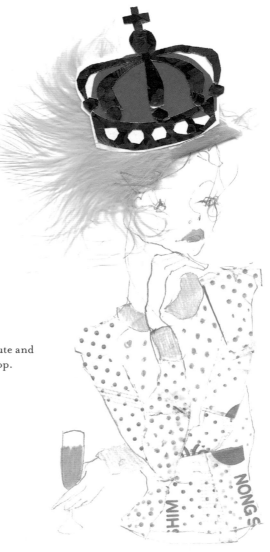

KIR ROYALE

Champagne flute

INGREDIENTS

1 oz. crème de cassis
5 oz. Champagne

METHOD

Pour crème de cassis into a flute and
gently pour Champagne on top.

CHAMPAGNE ROYALE
Champagne flute

INGREDIENTS
splash of black raspberry liqueur
6 oz. Champagne
fresh raspberries to garnish

METHOD
Pour liqueur into a flute, then slowly fill with Champagne. Garnish with raspberries.

MARTINI ROYALE
Martini glass

INGREDIENTS
3 oz. chilled vodka or gin
3 oz. Champagne

METHOD
Pour vodka or gin into a chilled martini glass and top with Champagne.

FRAISE DE CHAMPAGNE

Champagne flute

INGREDIENTS

3½ oz. Champagne
1 oz. crème de fraise des bois
1 tbsp. cognac

METHOD

Combine ingredients in a Champagne
flute and serve.

LEMON CELEBRATION

Champagne flute

INGREDIENTS

1 oz. black raspberry liqueur
1 oz. Bacardi Limon
3 oz. Champagne

METHOD

Shake ingredients gently with ice
(the Champagne will fizz).
Strain into a Champagne flute.

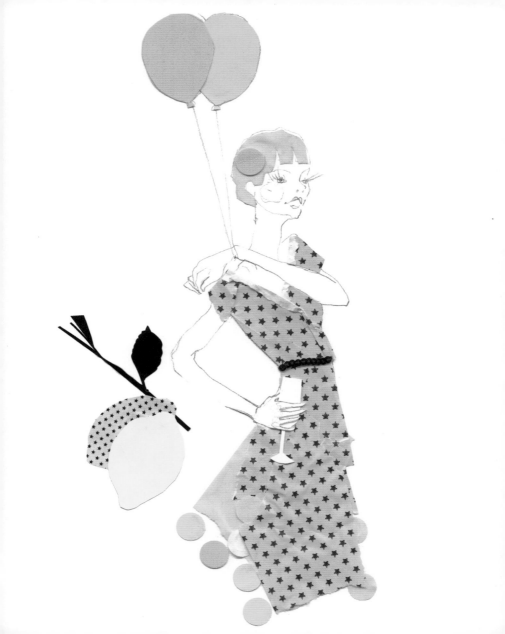

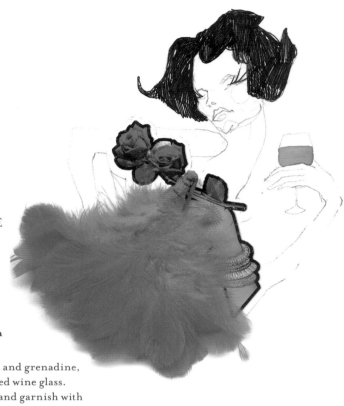

AMERICAN ROSE
Wine glass

INGREDIENTS
1½ oz. brandy
½ tsp. Pernod
1 tsp. grenadine
3 oz. Champagne
peach slice to garnish

METHOD
Shake brandy, Pernod and grenadine,
and strain into a chilled wine glass.
Fill with Champagne and garnish with
a peach slice.

CAMPARI CHAMPAGNE

Champagne flute

INGREDIENTS

1 oz. Campari
4 oz. Champagne
twist of lemon peel to garnish

METHOD

Pour Campari into a flute and fill
with Champagne. Twist the lemon
peel over the drink and serve.

A GOODNIGHT KISS

Champagne flute

INGREDIENTS

drop of Angostura bitters
sugar cube
4 oz. Champagne
splash of Campari

METHOD

Place a drop of Angostura bitters on
a sugar cube and set in a Champagne
flute. Add Champagne and Campari.

sipping at the sin palace

Gin sounds so old-fashioned, doesn't it? It's so proper and prim-school like. If it had a wardrobe it would be full of pleated skirts and ruffled shirts, lots of tweed and brooches. If gin were a girl she'd come across a little bashful and not quite willing to explore her princess qualities—but if she only knew what was hiding under her petticoat. She's a little prudish, but there's a diva dying for exposure underneath that veil of reservation.

If gin were a literary club, it would be packed with Emily Brontë and Jane Austen bookworms. Gin is for hopeless romantics, clinging to the ideal of Heathcliff waiting out yonder to take them away.

The gin and tonic is a classic drink—so ladylike, so petal-sweet and mildly snobbish. After a starring appearance in the mid-century as an oh-so-stylish martini, gin disappeared for a while. But now this spirit has been ripped away from its mothballs to seduce a whole new generation.

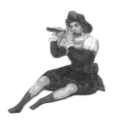

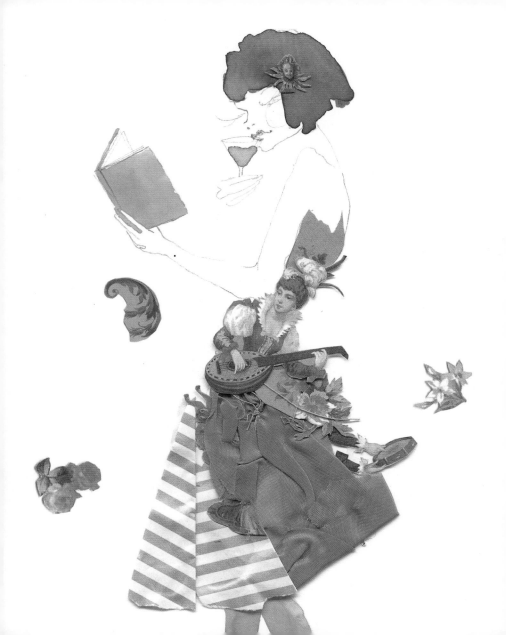

EMMA PEEL MARTINI
Martini glass

INGREDIENTS
1 oz. gin
½ oz. apple schnapps
½ oz. watermelon liqueur
½ oz. apple juice
½ oz. watermelon juice
apple peel to garnish

METHOD
Shake and strain all ingredients into
a chilled martini glass. Garnish with
green apple spiral (left floating).

CIN GIN
Martini glass

INGREDIENTS
½ cinnamon stick
splash of pineapple juice
2 oz. gin
1 tsp. lemongrass and ginger tea
cinnamon stick to garnish

METHOD
Muddle cinnamon with pineapple juice,
then add gin and ice. Shake and strain.
Serve in a martini glass laced with
lemongrass and ginger tea. Garnish
with cinnamon stick.

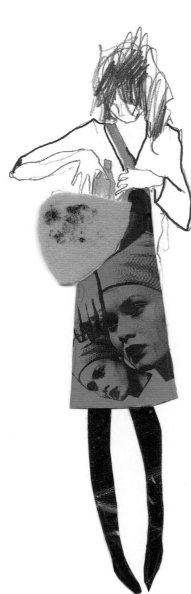

BOMBAY SCHMINT

Martini glass

INGREDIENTS
6 mint leaves
2 oz. gin
½ oz. crème de peche
dash of orange juice
sprig of mint to garnish

METHOD
Muddle mint leaves. Combine with other ingredients, shake and strain into a martini glass. Garnish with a mint sprig.

GIN GARDEN
Martini glass

INGREDIENTS
2–3 chunks cucumber
½ oz. elderflower cordial
1½ oz. gin
1½ oz. apple juice
cucumber slice to garnish

METHOD
Muddle cucumber with elderflower
cordial. Shake with remaining
ingredients and serve straight up in
a chilled martini glass. Garnish with
a cucumber slice.

ALOE VERA MARTINI
Martini glass

INGREDIENTS
2 oz. gin
½ oz. aloe vera water
½ oz. crème de peche
twist of orange to garnish

METHOD
Shake and strain all ingredients
into a martini glass. Garnish with
a twist of orange.

CAMPANA
Martini glass

INGREDIENTS
1 oz. gin
½ oz. Campari
½ oz. sweet vermouth
2 tsp. lime juice
½ oz. sugar syrup
slice of lime to garnish

METHOD
Shake and strain all ingredients into
a chilled martini glass then garnish
with a slice of lime.

CLASSIC MARTINI

Martini glass

INGREDIENTS

1½ oz. gin
1 tsp. dry vermouth
cocktail olive to garnish

METHOD

Stir gin and vermouth with ice cubes
in a mixing glass until chilled. Then
strain into a chilled martini glass.
Garnish with a cocktail olive.

POMEGRANATE MARTINI

Martini glass

INGREDIENTS

4 tbsp. pomegranate seeds
mint leaf
2 tsp. passionfruit puree
2 oz. gin
1 tsp. grenadine

METHOD

Muddle pomegranate, mint and puree,
add gin and grenadine, shake and
double-strain into a martini glass.

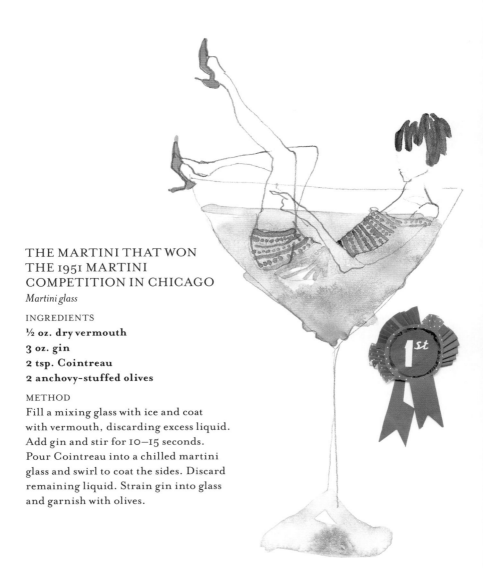

THE MARTINI THAT WON THE 1951 MARTINI COMPETITION IN CHICAGO

Martini glass

INGREDIENTS

½ oz. dry vermouth
3 oz. gin
2 tsp. Cointreau
2 anchovy-stuffed olives

METHOD

Fill a mixing glass with ice and coat with vermouth, discarding excess liquid. Add gin and stir for 10–15 seconds. Pour Cointreau into a chilled martini glass and swirl to coat the sides. Discard remaining liquid. Strain gin into glass and garnish with olives.

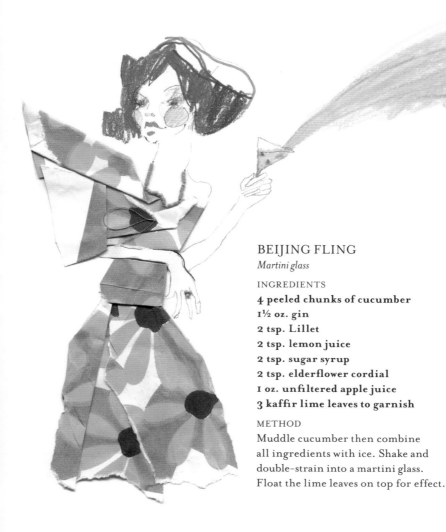

BEIJING FLING
Martini glass

INGREDIENTS
4 peeled chunks of cucumber
1½ oz. gin
2 tsp. Lillet
2 tsp. lemon juice
2 tsp. sugar syrup
2 tsp. elderflower cordial
1 oz. unfiltered apple juice
3 kaffir lime leaves to garnish

METHOD
Muddle cucumber then combine
all ingredients with ice. Shake and
double-strain into a martini glass.
Float the lime leaves on top for effect.

SINGAPORE SLING
Collins glass

INGREDIENTS
1 oz. gin
1½ oz. sour mix
½ oz. grenadine
splash of soda water
dash of cherry brandy

METHOD
Fill a shaker with ice, add all
ingredients (except soda water and
brandy). Shake well. Strain into an
ice-filled Collins glass, top with
soda water and float the cherry
brandy on top.

GIN SLING
Martini glass

INGREDIENTS
1 oz. gin
½ oz. sweet vermouth
½ oz. fresh lemon juice
½ oz. sugar syrup
dash of Angostura bitters
splash of soda water
lemon peel to garnish

METHOD
Shake all the ingredients (except the
soda water) with ice and strain into a
martini glass. Top with soda water.
Garnish with a spiral of lemon peel.

TOM COLLINS
Highball glass

INGREDIENTS

2 oz. gin
1½ oz. lemon juice
2 tsp. sugar syrup
splash of soda water

METHOD

Combine gin, juice and sugar syrup in a highball glass. Stir, add ice and fill with soda water.

SOUTHERN BELLE
Martini glass

INGREDIENTS

1½ oz. gin
½ oz. Aperol
1 oz. lime juice
1 tsp. sugar syrup
twist of lime to garnish

METHOD

Shake and strain all ingredients into a martini glass. Garnish with a twist of lime.

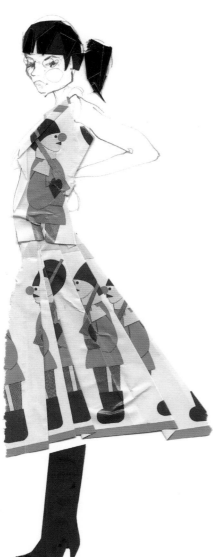

LONDON SUMMER
Tumbler

INGREDIENTS
½ kiwi fruit
½ small lime
pinch of raw sugar
1 oz. gin
2 tsp. black raspberry liqueur

METHOD
Muddle fruit and sugar in a tumbler.
Add ice and crush with other ingredients.

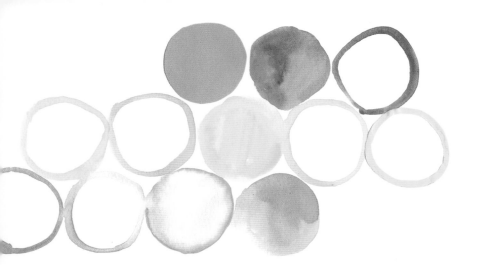

HULA HOOP
Martini glass

INGREDIENTS
2 oz. gin
I oz. orange juice
½ oz. pineapple juice
cherry to garnish

METHOD
Shake all the ingredients with ice and
strain into a martini glass. Garnish
with a cherry.

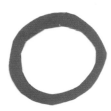

CORINTHIAN ICED TEA
Bamboo glass

INGREDIENTS
I½ oz. gin
½ oz. crème de pomme verte
I oz. white cranberry juice
2 tsp. lemon juice
2 tsp. sugar syrup
2 tsp. cranberry syrup
4 watermelon chunks
8 mint leaves
½ oz. rosehip and hibiscus tea
wedge of watermelon to garnish

METHOD
Combine all ingredients (except tea)
in a shaker with ice. Shake and pour
into a bamboo glass, then top with tea and
crushed ice. Serve with a long straw and
garnish with a thin watermelon wedge.

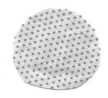

ALICE SPRINGS

Highball glass

INGREDIENTS

2 oz. gin
½ oz. lemon juice
½ oz. orange juice
½ tsp. grenadine
3 dashes of Angostura bitters
splash of soda water
½ orange slice to garnish

METHOD

Shake all ingredients (except soda water)
with ice. Pour into a highball glass and
fill with soda. Garnish with orange slice.

SOUTH PAW

Highball glass

INGREDIENTS

1 oz. gin
½ oz. Campari
splash of sparkling grapefruit juice
2 wedges of fresh lime to garnish

METHOD

Build ingredients in a highball glass
over ice. Garnish with lime wedges.

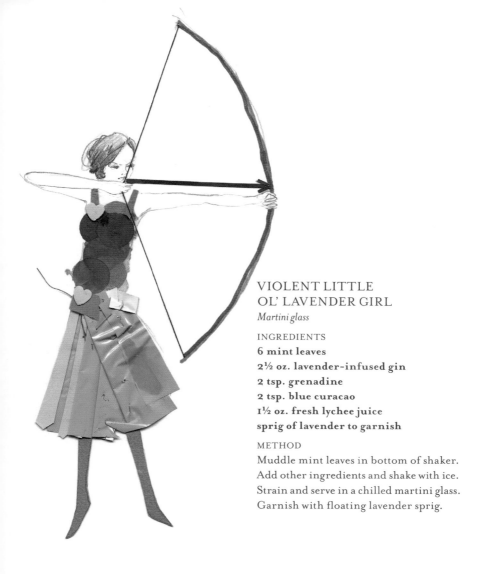

VIOLENT LITTLE OL' LAVENDER GIRL

Martini glass

INGREDIENTS

6 mint leaves
2½ oz. lavender-infused gin
2 tsp. grenadine
2 tsp. blue curacao
1½ oz. fresh lychee juice
sprig of lavender to garnish

METHOD

Muddle mint leaves in bottom of shaker.
Add other ingredients and shake with ice.
Strain and serve in a chilled martini glass.
Garnish with floating lavender sprig.

GIMLET

Martini glass

INGREDIENTS

1½ oz. gin
2 tsp. lime juice
wedge of lime to garnish

METHOD

Shake gin and lime juice in a shaker
with ice and strain into a martini glass.
Garnish with a lime wedge.

COLAZIONE

Martini glass

INGREDIENTS

3 chunks of grapefruit
2 tsp. raw sugar
1½ oz. gin
2 tsp. Campari
½ oz. crème de peche
grapefruit peel to garnish

METHOD

Muddle grapefruit with sugar, then
shake with other ingredients and
double-strain into a martini glass.
Garnish with a flamed grapefruit peel.

QUINTINI
Martini glass

INGREDIENTS

1½ oz. gin
2 tsp. Lillet
½ oz. quince liqueur
dash of orange bitters
shaved orange zest to garnish

METHOD

Shake and strain all ingredients into a martini glass. Garnish with orange zest.

MILLER'S MARTINI
Martini glass

INGREDIENTS

2 oz. gin
dash of Grand Marnier
dash of orange bitters
mint leaf to garnish

METHOD

Shake and strain all ingredients into a martini glass. Garnish with a floating mint leaf.

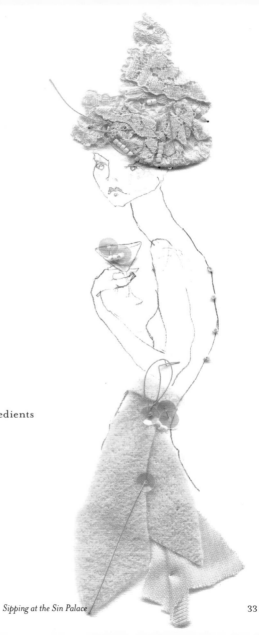

VANILLA KISS
Martini glass

INGREDIENTS
1 oz. gin
½ oz. crème de cacao
½ oz. butterscotch schnapps
sugar to garnish

METHOD
Shake and double-strain all ingredients
into a chilled martini glass with
sugar-crusted rim.

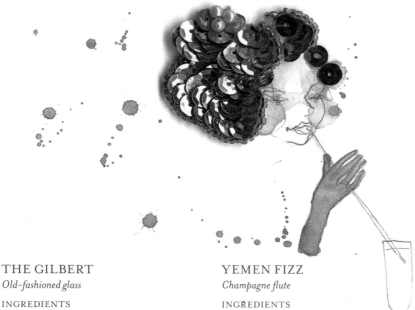

THE GILBERT
Old-fashioned glass

INGREDIENTS
handful of white grapes
2 slices of ginger
1 oz. sloe gin
2 tsp. crème de gingembre
1 tsp. black raspberry liqueur
½ oz. Jaggard lemon myrtle
1 tsp. sour mix
grapes to garnish

METHOD
Muddle small handful of grapes
and slices of ginger. Shake with other
ingredients and strain into an
old-fashioned glass. Garnish with
three skewered grapes.

YEMEN FIZZ
Champagne flute

INGREDIENTS
4 red grapes
½ oz. gin
2 tsp. crème de cassis
5 oz. Champagne
extra grape to garnish

METHOD
Muddle grapes. Shake all ingredients
and strain into a flute. Top with
Champagne and float a small red grape.

K.G.B.

Martini glass

INGREDIENTS

2 oz. gin
1 oz. kirsch
1 oz. apricot brandy
½ oz. lemon juice
1 tsp. superfine sugar
twist of lemon to garnish

METHOD

Shake all ingredients with ice and strain into a martini glass. Garnish with lemon twist.

TINA'S ON A TAIPEI BUS

Highball glass

INGREDIENTS

1 oz. rose petal–infused gin
1 oz. vodka
½ oz. watermelon liqueur
2 tsp. crème de gingembre
6 drops of rose water
2½ oz. pink grapefruit juice
1 tsp. parfait amour
rose petals to garnish

METHOD

Build all ingredients (except parfait amour) in a highball glass over cubed ice. Stir gently. Float parfait amour over top. Garnish with rose petals.

rum like you stole something

As the signature drop of the tropics, rum can bring out the drunken sailor girl in everyone. Fueled by mischievous Caribbean libido, this frisky spirit locates the flirt within and teaches us to run with tomfoolery. It conjures sweeping white beaches, tiny polka-dot bikinis and Tiki-decorated shacks with slow-revolving fans. It's a laid-back sip that washes away the stress of everyday life, taking us to a tropical stopover, even if just for a moment.

Rum is for the armchair adventurer who sports a piña colada (not milk) mustache and thinks mint leaves are strictly for mojitos (never for cooking). It's for grass-skirted babes who pin flowers in their hair, hold exquisite cocktails and know how to have fun—whether it's under a palm tree or in an urban bar.

The Mai Tai is an old favorite, but to really share the wealth, a good summer punch is in order. Mix up a batch and demand that your friends take part in the escapades, scooping mouthfuls of fruity rum flavors until sunlight ebbs away and the hammock beckons.

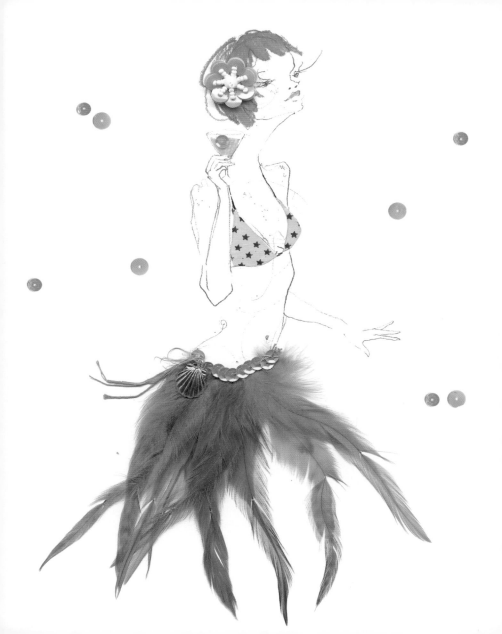

FUNKY CARIBBEAN

Martini glass

INGREDIENTS

1½ oz. vanilla-infused rum
1½ oz. sauvignon blanc
1½ oz. pineapple juice
½ oz. sugar syrup
vanilla bean to garnish

METHOD

Shake and strain all ingredients into
a chilled martini glass. Garnish with
a split vanilla bean.

CARAMELIZED FIG & BANANA DAIQUIRI

Martini glass

INGREDIENTS

1½ oz. rum
2 tsp. Licor 43
2 tsp. butterscotch schnapps
½ oz. fig puree
2 tsp. lemon juice
2 tbsp. caramelized banana
caramelized fig to garnish

METHOD

Blend all ingredients with ice and serve
in a martini glass. Add two short straws
and garnish with caramelized fig.

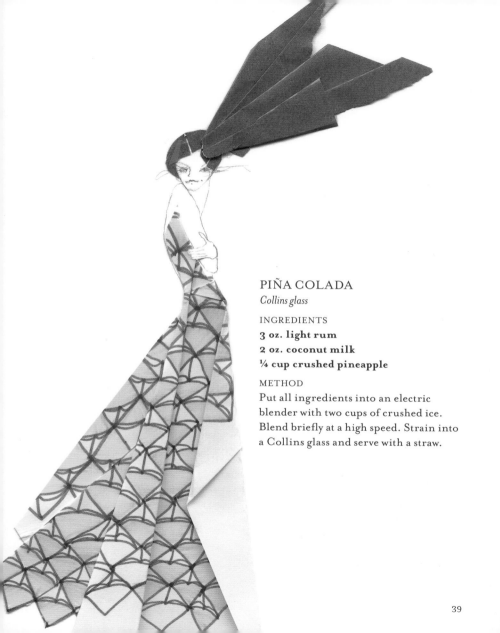

PIÑA COLADA
Collins glass

INGREDIENTS
3 oz. light rum
2 oz. coconut milk
¼ cup crushed pineapple

METHOD
Put all ingredients into an electric
blender with two cups of crushed ice.
Blend briefly at a high speed. Strain into
a Collins glass and serve with a straw.

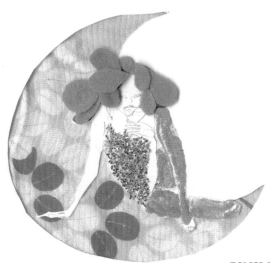

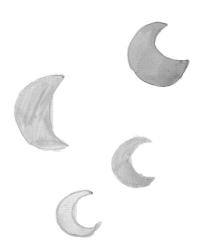

PINK MOON

Martini glass

INGREDIENTS

1½ oz. white rum
2 tsp. Licor 43
1 tsp. vanilla syrup
½ lime
½ oz. pink grapefruit juice
twist of lemon to garnish

METHOD

Shake ingredients and pour into
a martini glass. Garnish with a
lemon twist.

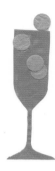

LAWRENCE ICED T.E.
Bamboo glass

INGREDIENTS

I oz. rum
½ oz. cherry liqueur
½ oz. peach liqueur
I oz. peach tea
I oz. cranberry juice
½ oz. lemon juice
I tsp. sugar syrup
I oz. apricot puree
2 thin slices of red chili to garnish

METHOD

Combine all ingredients with ice then shake and pour into a bamboo glass. Top with crushed ice. Garnish with chili and serve with a long straw.

ALOHA SCREWDRIVER
Goblet

INGREDIENTS

½ oz. coconut-flavored rum
I oz. vodka
2 oz. orange juice
2 oz. pineapple juice
2 maraschino cherries to garnish

METHOD

Blend all ingredients with crushed ice until smooth. Pour into a chilled goblet and garnish with maraschino cherries.

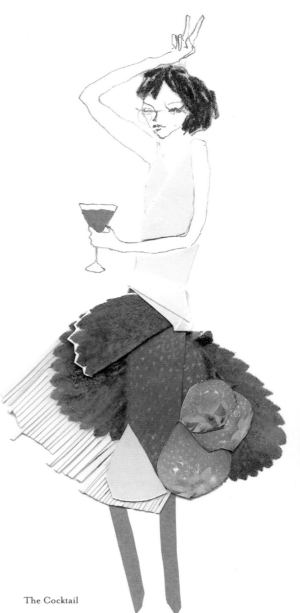

STRAWBERRY DAIQUIRI

Martini glass

INGREDIENTS

1 oz. strawberries
½ oz. strawberry schnapps
1 oz. light rum
1 oz. lime juice
1 tsp. superfine sugar

METHOD

Muddle strawberries. Shake all
ingredients with ice, strain into
a martini glass and serve.

ZANZIBAR
Highball glass

INGREDIENTS

3 blueberries
3 strawberries
1 oz. vanilla-infused rum
1 oz. passionfruit liqueur
2 wedges of lime
3 oz. cranberry juice

METHOD

Muddle blueberries and strawberries. Pour into a highball glass with alcohol over crushed ice. Add wedges of fresh lime and finish with cranberry juice.

MOJITO
Highball glass

INGREDIENTS

5 mint leaves
½ cup fresh chopped lime
2 oz. white rum
½ oz. sugar syrup
1 tbsp. superfine sugar
splash of soda water
sprig of mint to garnish

METHOD

Muddle mint leaves and fresh lime (with peel). Shake with rum, syrup and sugar, and pour into a highball glass. Top with soda water and garnish with a sprig of mint.

YACHT CLUB PUNCH

Collins glass

INGREDIENTS

1 oz. banana-flavored rum
1 oz. scotch whiskey
3 oz. orange or pineapple juice
splash of soda water
maraschino cherry and slice of
orange to garnish

METHOD

Fill shaker with ice, add ingredients
(except soda water) and shake well.
Pour into Collins glass and fill with
soda. Garnish with maraschino cherry
and orange slice.

A DAY OFF

Tumbler

INGREDIENTS

1 lime
1 oz. Aperol
½ oz. dark rum
2 tsp. lychee liqueur
splash of unfiltered apple juice
basil leaf to garnish

METHOD

Slice lime into quarters and mix
with Aperol, rum, liqueur and ice.
Top with apple juice. Garnish with
fresh basil leaf.

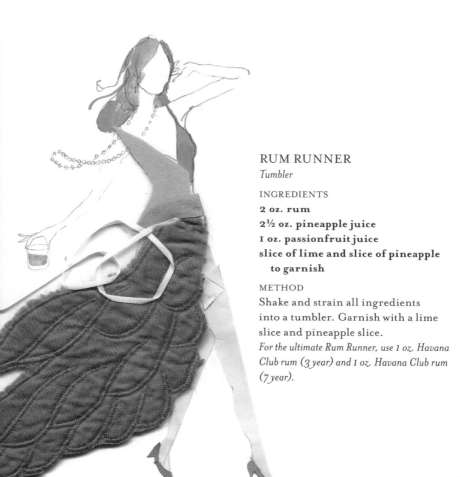

RUM RUNNER
Tumbler

INGREDIENTS
2 oz. rum
2½ oz. pineapple juice
1 oz. passionfruit juice
slice of lime and slice of pineapple
**   to garnish**

METHOD
Shake and strain all ingredients
into a tumbler. Garnish with a lime
slice and pineapple slice.
For the ultimate Rum Runner, use 1 oz. Havana
Club rum (3 year) and 1 oz. Havana Club rum
(7 year).

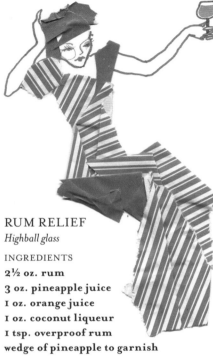

RUM RELIEF
Highball glass

INGREDIENTS

2½ oz. rum
3 oz. pineapple juice
I oz. orange juice
I oz. coconut liqueur
I tsp. overproof rum
wedge of pineapple to garnish

METHOD

Shake and strain all ingredients
(except overproof rum) into a highball
glass. Float overproof rum and garnish
with a pineapple wedge.

RED RUM
Martini glass

INGREDIENTS

I oz. rum
I oz. Cinzano Rosso
2 tsp. maraschino juice
dash of Angostura bitters
twist of orange to garnish

METHOD

Combine all ingredients, stir and
strain into a chilled martini glass.
Garnish with an orange twist.

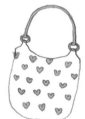

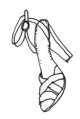

TIKI MAI TAI

Hurricane glass

INGREDIENTS

1½ oz. rum
1 oz. hazelnut liqueur
¾ oz. triple sec
1 oz. pineapple juice
1 oz. sweet and sour mix

METHOD

Blend all ingredients with 3 oz. ice until smooth. Pour into a chilled hurricane glass.

HURRICANE

Martini glass

INGREDIENTS

1 oz. white rum
1 oz. dark rum
1 tsp. passionfruit syrup
½ oz. lime juice

METHOD

Shake all ingredients with ice and strain into a martini glass.

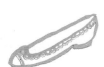

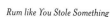

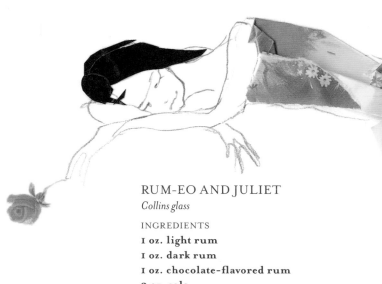

RUM-EO AND JULIET
Collins glass

INGREDIENTS
1 oz. light rum
1 oz. dark rum
1 oz. chocolate-flavored rum
3 oz. cola
½ oz. 151-proof rum
slice of lemon to garnish

METHOD
Fill a chilled Collins glass with ice and add
light, dark and chocolate rums. Top with
cola and stir gently. Float 151-proof rum.
Garnish with a slice of lemon.

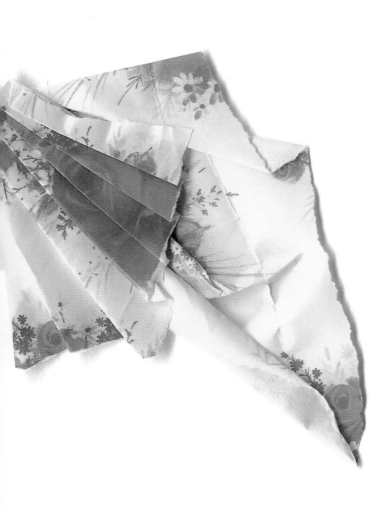

sake in the city

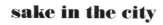

It's an ancient drop (more than 6,000 years old, in fact), but the sake trend is finally catching on. These fancy drinks are for women keen to try something different, who like variations on the classics and are ready for a neon-lit Tokyo experience without leaving their bar stools. It's for those wannabe Sofia Coppolas lusting after *Lost in Translation* moments—where fast-paced living and language barriers confuse the taste buds and kooky pop culture sits happily alongside geisha grace.

Sake suits the karaoke queen who adores the spotlight but is also ideal for the occasional tippler looking for a low-alcoholic drink. And sake is just that—a popular, mild-flavored spirit that doesn't contain sulfites (those nasties that contribute to hangovers). Isn't that thoughtful? It's becoming increasingly popular to substitute sake for gin and vodka in classic cocktails, such as Martinis and Cosmopolitans.

Tonight, play the devious hostess and free yourself of predictability. It may be a long way to the top if you want to rock and roll, but it's a mere hop, skip and a jump away from a top night with this Japanese delicacy.

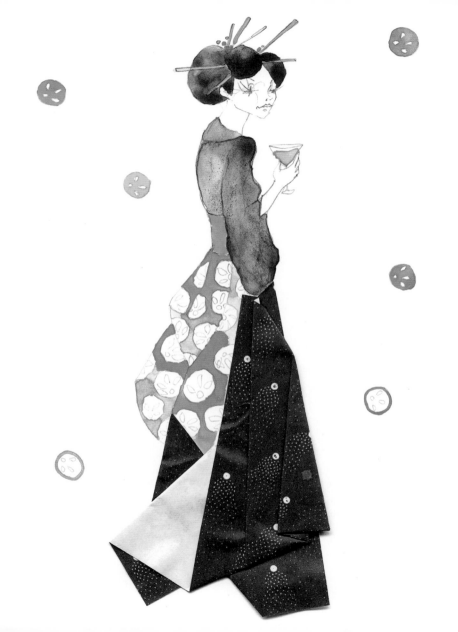

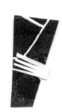

KYOTO PROTOCOL
Martini glass

INGREDIENTS

½ kiwi fruit

⅓ small cucumber

½ oz. lime juice

1 oz. unfiltered apple juice

½ oz. sake

1 oz. white rum

½ oz. crème de pomme verte

2 tsp. kiwi syrup

METHOD

Muddle kiwi and cucumber. Add juices,
then alcohol. Add ice, shake and
double-strain into a martini glass.

SAKETINI

Martini glass

INGREDIENTS

dash of dry vermouth
3 oz. chili-infused sake
anchovy-stuffed olive to garnish

METHOD

Wash ice with vermouth and strain
thoroughly. Add sake, gently stir and
strain into a martini glass. Garnish
with anchovy-stuffed olive.

W BAR SAKETINI

Martini glass

INGREDIENTS

1 oz. sake
1½ oz. vodka
½ oz. Midori
1 oz. lemon juice
2 tsp. sugar syrup
sugar to garnish

METHOD

Shake and strain all ingredients into
a sugar-crusted martini glass.

42 FLYING MULES
Highball glass

INGREDIENTS
½ lime
6 torn mint leaves
½ large Thai chili
1 oz. sake
1 oz. vodka
2 tsp. lemon juice
splash of ginger ale
sprig of mint to garnish

METHOD
In a shaker, muddle lime, mint and
chili. Add sake, vodka, lemon juice and
ice, then shake. Pour into a highball
glass and top with ginger ale. Garnish
with a fresh mint sprig.

AUTUMN THUNDER
Highball glass

INGREDIENTS
1 oz. sake
½ oz. black raspberry liqueur
½ oz. Cointreau
1 oz. orange juice
1 oz. pineapple juice
½ oz. lime juice
½ oz. Benedictine
dash of Angostura bitters
twists of lemon and orange to garnish

METHOD
Place all ingredients in shaker and
mix well. Strain into a highball glass
filled with ice and serve. Garnish with
interlinked orange and lemon twists.

BLOODY MARY
Highball glass

INGREDIENTS
dash of Worcestershire sauce
dash of Tabasco sauce
pinch of wasabi paste
2 tsp. lemon juice
3 oz. tomato juice
1½ oz. sake
½ oz. vodka
celery stalk
freshly cracked black pepper to garnish

METHOD
Pour Worcestershire and Tabasco sauces
into shaker, add wasabi and lemon and
tomato juices. Shake and strain into
a highball glass containing sake, vodka
and celery. Crack pepper on top.

GINGER CHAN
Highball glass

INGREDIENTS
1½ oz. ginger-infused sake
juice of ½ lime
1 oz. apple juice
6 mint leaves
splash of ginger ale

METHOD
Shake sake, juices and mint, then pour
into a highball glass full of ice. Top with
ginger ale.

ANGEL TSUZI
Martini glass

INGREDIENTS
1 oz. sake
2 tsp. orgeat syrup
½ oz. Frangelico
1 oz. half and half
ground cinnamon to garnish

METHOD
Combine all ingredients with ice.
Shake and strain into a martini glass.
Garnish with freshly ground cinnamon.

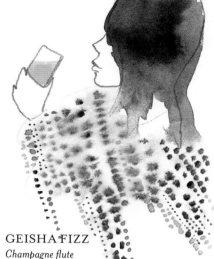

LYCHEE MARTINI
Martini glass

INGREDIENTS
1 oz. sherry
5 oz. cachaça
½ oz. sake
1 oz. lychee syrup
1 tsp. elderflower cordial
stalk of lemongrass to garnish

METHOD
Shake and strain all ingredients into
a chilled martini glass. Garnish with
lemongrass stalk.

GEISHA FIZZ
Champagne flute

INGREDIENTS
2 lychees
2 tsp. lemon juice
½ oz. sake
4 oz. Champagne
½ oz. crème de gingembre
kaffir lime leaf to garnish

METHOD
Muddle lychees and lemon juice.
Combine all ingredients with ice in
a shaker. Shake and strain into a flute.
Garnish with a broken kaffir lime leaf.
Crème de gingembre is a French ginger liqueur.

J-POP

Martini glass

INGREDIENTS

3 slices ginger
3 slices Asian pear
1½ oz. sake
½ oz. feijoa vodka
1½ oz. pear liqueur
2 tsp. honey
½ oz. unfiltered apple juice
slice of Asian pear to garnish

METHOD

Muddle ginger and Asian pear.
Combine with other ingredients,
shake and double-strain into a
martini glass. Garnish with a slice
of Asian pear.

JAPANESE PEAR

Martini glass

INGREDIENTS

¼ Asian pear
½ oz. sake
1½ oz. vodka
½ oz. apple liqueur
2 tsp. lemon juice
2 tsp. pear liqueur
1 tsp. sugar
slice of pear to garnish

METHOD

Muddle Asian pear then combine with
other ingredients. Shake and strain into
a martini glass. Garnish with a pear slice.

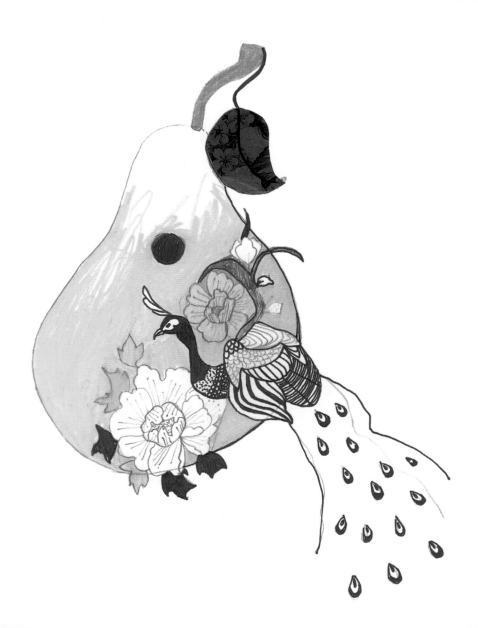

the tequila made me do it

If you're up for a big night, then tequila is your not-so-trusty companion. This clear spirit can light you up like a piñata at Carnaval. But friends, beware—one hit too many and a blindfolded demon will take a swing, splitting you clean in two. And before you can cry "ole!" you'll find yourself on a cold concrete floor somewhere in Mexico City on Constable Pedro's wanted list.

Tequila is for girls who know how to party—it has La Bamba written all over its spirited heart. The Margarita is the most popular use of tequila—it's a flirty one, perfect for loosening tongues, but keep in mind it's a lethal cocktail that goes down smoothly only to knock down the toughest of men.

So put on your best poncho, pin a red rose in your hair and dust on some bronzer. Tonight, señorita, is for making sweet, illicit love—time to be saucy and brazen because, after all, the tequila made you do it . . .

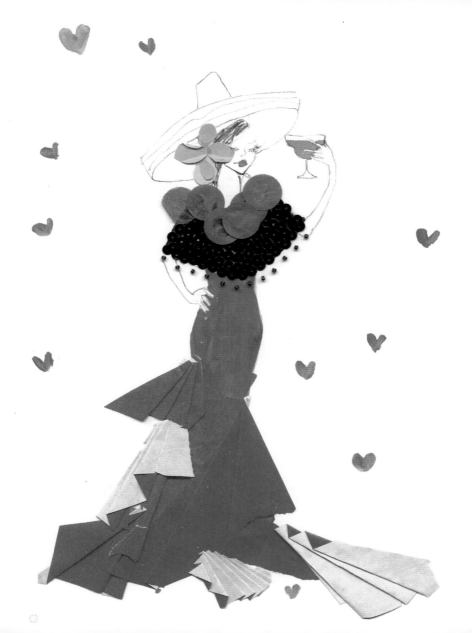

PASSIONFRUIT MARGARITA

Martini glass

INGREDIENTS

1½ oz. tequila
½ oz. triple sec
1 oz. lemon juice
1½ oz. passionfruit puree
salt to garnish

METHOD

Blend ingredients with ice. Serve in
a salt-crusted martini glass.

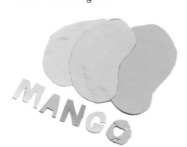

MANGO MARGARITA

Martini glass

INGREDIENTS

1½ oz. tequila
½ oz. triple sec
½ oz. lime juice
½ oz. lemon juice
¼ fresh mango in chunks
3 sour cherries to garnish

METHOD

Place all ingredients in a blender with
ice and puree. Pour into a martini glass.
Garnish with sour cherries.

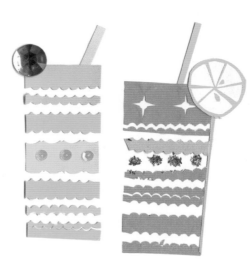

HOLA MAMASITA
Martini glass

INGREDIENTS

1 oz. kaffir lime–infused tequila
½ oz. passionfruit liqueur
½ oz. ginger liqueur
1 oz. passionfruit puree
ground cinnamon to garnish

METHOD

Shake and strain all ingredients into cinnamon-crusted martini glass.

TEQUILA SUNRISE
Highball glass

INGREDIENTS

1½ oz. tequila
½ tsp. lime juice
splash of orange juice
½ oz. grenadine

METHOD

Fill glass with ice; add tequila and lime juice and stir. Top with orange juice and trickle grenadine on top.

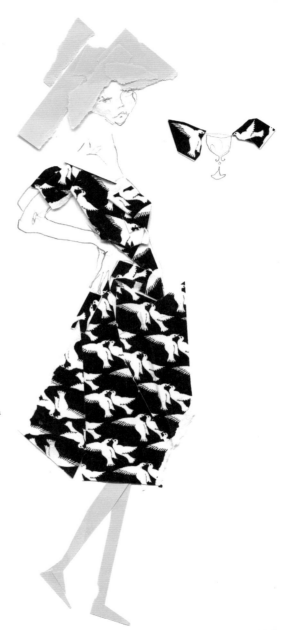

TEQUILA MOCKINGBIRD
Collins glass

INGREDIENTS

2 oz. tequila
1 oz. triple sec
3 oz. pineapple juice
maraschino cherry to garnish

METHOD

Shake ingredients with ice and strain
into a Collins glass. Garnish with
a maraschino cherry.

TO KILL A ROSE
Martini glass

INGREDIENTS

1½ oz. raspberry puree
1½ oz. heavy cream
½ oz. crème de framboise
4 tsp. superfine sugar
2 oz. rose and berry–infused tequila
dash of rose syrup
rose petals to garnish

METHOD

Heat puree, cream and crème de framboise with sugar in a frying pan for 30 seconds on a high flame. Add tequila and stir. Pour into a martini glass, add rose syrup and garnish with two rose petals.

LOLITA
Martini glass

INGREDIENTS

½ oz. tequila
2 tsp. lime juice
1 tsp. honey
2 dashes of Angostura bitters

METHOD

Shake all ingredients and strain into a martini glass. Serve with a couple of ice cubes.

lolita

MEXICAN ROSE
Tumbler

INGREDIENTS
½ oz. tequila
2 tsp. strawberry schnapps
1½ oz. milk
½ oz. grenadine

METHOD
Shake all ingredients and strain into
a tumbler.

MEXICAN MANHATTAN
Martini glass

INGREDIENTS
1½ oz. tequila
2 tsp. maraschino juice
2 tsp. sweet vermouth
2–3 dashes of orange bitters
cherry to garnish

METHOD
Stir all ingredients and serve straight-
up in a chilled martini glass. Garnish
with a cherry (or maraschino when not
in season).

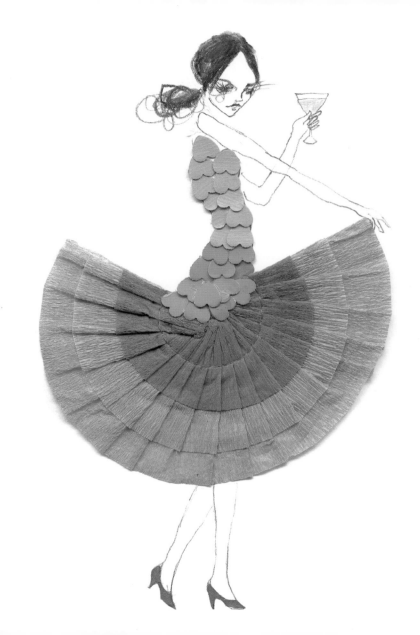

WATERMELON & CORIANDER MARGARITA

Margarita glass

INGREDIENTS

4 chunks of watermelon
2 tsp. lemon juice
1½ oz. tequila
2 tsp. Midori
2 tsp. sugar syrup
dash of ground coriander
6 coriander leaves
extra coriander leaf to garnish

METHOD

Muddle watermelon and lemon juice.
Then combine all ingredients in a shaker
with ice. Shake and double-strain into
a margarita glass. Float a coriander leaf.

PEPPERED STRAWBERRY MARGARITA

Martini glass

INGREDIENTS

3–4 strawberries
1½ oz. pepper-infused tequila
½ oz. crème de fraise
1 oz. lime juice
dash of sugar syrup
cracked pepper and extra strawberry
to garnish

METHOD

Muddle strawberries. Add remaining
ingredients, then shake. Serve straight up
in a chilled martini glass. Garnish with
a cracked pepper rim, pepper dusting
and a speared strawberry quarter.

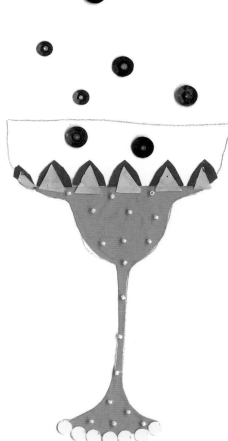

ARABIAN MARGARITA
Margarita glass

INGREDIENTS

1½ oz. cardamon-infused tequila
½ oz. apricot brandy
1½ oz. apricot puree
½ oz. lemon juice
1 tsp. sugar syrup
dried apricot to garnish

METHOD

Pour all ingredients into a shaker
with ice. Shake and strain into a
margarita glass. Float a dried apricot.

W BAR MARGARITA
Martini glass

INGREDIENTS
1½ oz. pepper-infused tequila
½ oz. triple sec
1 oz. lime juice
dash of sugar syrup
cracked pepper to garnish

METHOD
Shake all ingredients and serve
straight up in a martini glass.
Garnish with a cracked pepper rim
and a pepper dusting.

LIME STREET MARGARITA
Margarita glass

INGREDIENTS
½ mandarin, peeled
2 tsp. lime juice
2 tsp. lemon juice
1½ oz. tequila
½ oz. mandarin liqueur
2 tsp. sugar syrup
4 raspberries
salt to garnish

METHOD
Muddle mandarin with lime and
lemon juices. Combine all ingredients
with ice, shake and strain into a half
salt-encrusted margarita glass.

BLUE MARGARITA
Martini glass

INGREDIENTS
1½ oz. tequila
½ oz. Grand Marnier
1 oz. blue curacao
1 oz. lime juice
dash of sugar syrup
salt to garnish

METHOD
Shake all ingredients with ice.
Strain into a salt-crusted martini glass.

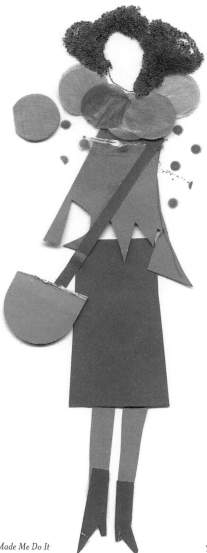

HIMALAYA
Martini glass

INGREDIENTS

⅓ Asian pear
2 tsp. lemon juice
I oz. tequila
½ oz. chamomile liqueur
2 tsp. green apple liqueur
I tsp. caramel liqueur
I tsp. cinnamon syrup
slice of Asian pear to garnish

METHOD

Muddle pear and lemon juice in a
mixing glass. Combine with other
ingredients and ice and shake.
Double-strain into a martini glass.
Garnish with a slice of Asian pear.

SCIMITAR

Martini glass

INGREDIENTS

I oz. tequila
I oz. Licor 43
I oz. espresso
kiwi slice to garnish

METHOD

Pour all ingredients into a mixing
glass with ice. Shake and double-strain
into a martini glass. Garnish with a kiwi
slice skewer.

EL STAMOSA

Martini glass

INGREDIENTS

¼ green apple
¼ fresh peach
3 wedges of lime
2 tsp. peach puree
I½ oz. kaffir lime–infused tequila
2 tsp. green apple liqueur
½ oz. Nothing liqueur (optional)
I½ oz. apple juice
I tsp. sugar syrup
kaffir lime leaf to garnish

METHOD

Muddle fruit. Combine with remaining
ingredients, then shake and serve
straight up in a chilled martini glass.
Garnish with a floated kaffir lime leaf.

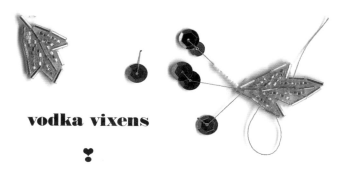

vodka vixens

❧

Depending on how and with whom you consume it, vodka can either be your one-way ticket to an Orwellian down-and-out-in-London experience, or make you feel like a Manhattanite flirting in the East Village all night long. It's an elegant drop, now infused with all manner of fruit to keep us guessing, but let it be known that vodka is for women who take risks—women who tease and conquer and command the attention of dangerous men.

Vodka is as racy as a Bond girl, as alluring as a 50s Hollywood starlet and as compelling as a KGB agent dabbling in a little Russian roulette. Most important, vodka is versatile,

adopting the flavor of whatever you choose to mix it with—it can seduce in the form of a Vodkatini or ease the pain as a Bloody Mary. It even captured the hearts of viewers worldwide as the cashed-up girls from *Sex and the City* downed Cosmopolitans aplenty.

Far from passé, vodka cocktails are part of the establishment when it comes to serious drinking. It's for every woman, from the peroxide blond, wannabe rocker hanging around bars to glimpse her favorite rock star to the couture princess who allures in less amplified ways.

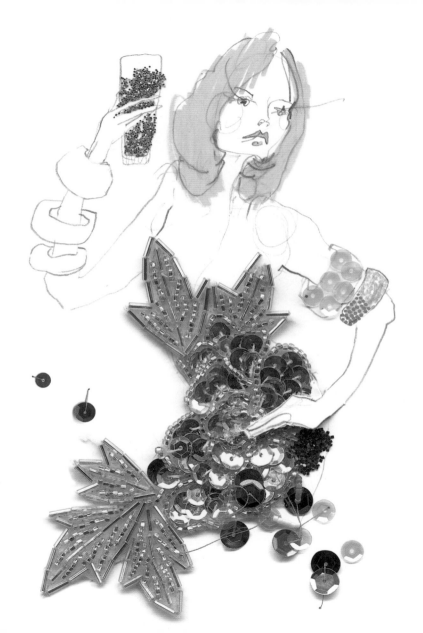

W BAR MARTINI

Martini glass

INGREDIENTS

1½ oz. vodka
2 tsp. black raspberry liqueur
2 tsp. anise liqueur
dash of cranberry juice
dash of lemon juice
dash of sugar syrup
cranberries and twist of lemon
   to garnish

METHOD

Shake all ingredients and strain into
a chilled martini glass. Garnish with
speared cranberries and a lemon twist.

CRANAPPLE MARTINI

Martini glass

INGREDIENTS

1 oz. citrus-infused vodka
1 oz. Cointreau
dash of ginger liqueur
1 oz. cranberry juice
1 oz. apple juice
½ fresh lime juice
splash of ginger ale
squeeze of lime and ginger slice
   to garnish

METHOD

Shake all ingredients and strain into
a chilled martini glass. Garnish with a
lime squeeze and a speared ginger slice.

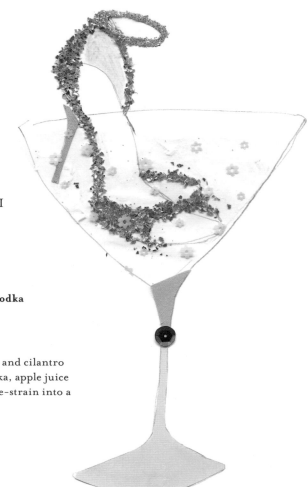

STILETTO MARTINI
Martini glass

INGREDIENTS
5 chunks of pineapple
sliver of ginger
4 cilantro leaves
2 oz. pineapple-infused vodka
½ oz. apple juice
2 tsp. almond syrup

METHOD
Muddle pineapple, ginger and cilantro
leaves. Combine with vodka, apple juice
and almond syrup. Double-strain into a
martini glass and serve.

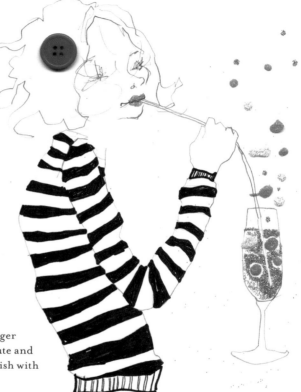

PEAR & GINGER FIZZ
Champagne flute

INGREDIENTS

1 oz. vodka
2 tsp. ginger liqueur
1 oz. pear nectar
splash of Champagne
slice of pear to garnish

METHOD

Shake and strain vodka, ginger
liqueur and nectar into a flute and
top with Champagne. Garnish with
a pear slice.

GINGER & LEMONGRASS MARTINI

Martini glass

INGREDIENTS
**½ inch slice of fresh lemongrass root
fine slice of ginger
2 oz. vodka
2 tsp. sugar syrup
strip of lemongrass to garnish**

METHOD
Muddle lemongrass and ginger.
Shake with vodka and sugar syrup and
double-strain into a martini glass.
Garnish with a lemongrass strip.

APPLE & CILANTRO MARTINI

Martini glass

INGREDIENTS
**½ Granny Smith apple
5 cilantro leaves
1½ oz. vodka
½ oz. crème de pomme verte
½ oz. clear apple juice
dash of lime juice
extra cilantro leaf to garnish**

METHOD
Muddle apple and cilantro.
Combine with alcohol. Shake and
strain into a martini glass. Float a
cilantro leaf on top.

SEABREEZE

Highball glass

INGREDIENTS

1½ oz. vodka
4 oz. cranberry juice
1 oz. grapefruit juice
wedge of lime to garnish

METHOD

Pour vodka and juice into a highball glass with ice and stir well. Garnish with a lime wedge.

CLASSIC BLOODY MARY

Highball glass

INGREDIENTS

2 oz. vodka
3 oz. tomato juice
½ oz. lemon juice
black pepper and salt
3 dashes of Worcestershire sauce
2 drops of Tabasco sauce
**wedge of lemon and celery stalk
    to garnish**

METHOD

Shake all ingredients with ice and strain into a highball glass over crushed ice. Garnish with a lemon wedge and celery stalk.

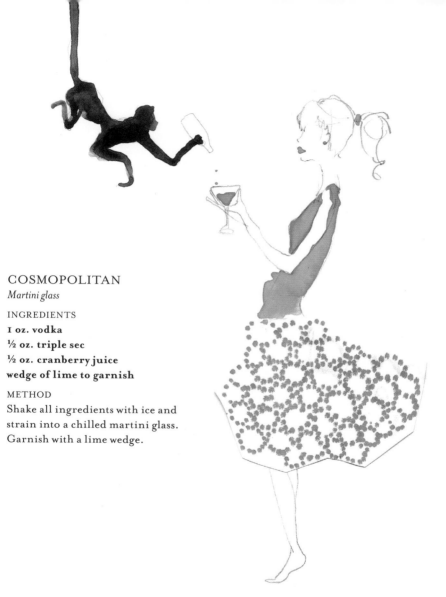

COSMOPOLITAN
Martini glass

INGREDIENTS
1 oz. vodka
½ oz. triple sec
½ oz. cranberry juice
wedge of lime to garnish

METHOD
Shake all ingredients with ice and
strain into a chilled martini glass.
Garnish with a lime wedge.

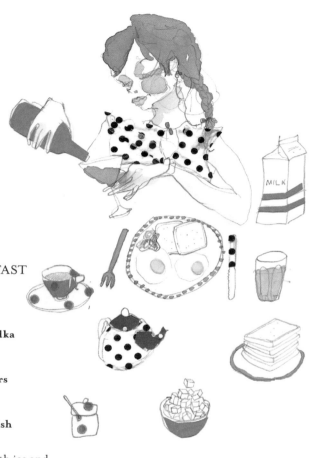

EASTERN BREAKFAST MARTINI

Martini glass

INGREDIENTS

1 oz. citrus-infused vodka
½ oz. quince liqueur
½ oz. Cointreau
2 drops of orange bitters
2 tsp. lemon juice
4 tsp. quince jam
twist of orange to garnish

METHOD

Shake all ingredients with ice and strain into a martini glass. Garnish with a twist of orange.

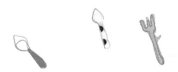

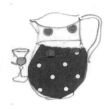

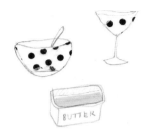

BAGHDAD ICED TEA
Bamboo glass

INGREDIENTS
¼ green apple
6 mint leaves
I oz. apple juice
½ oz. lime juice
I½ oz. vodka
½ oz. apple liqueur
I tsp. gin
2 tsp. rose syrup
½ oz. jasmine tea
2 slices of red chili to garnish

METHOD
Muddle apple, mint leaves, apple juice
and lime juice. Shake with vodka, liqueur,
gin, rose syrup and ice, and pour into a
bamboo glass. Top with tea and crushed
ice. Garnish with chili slices and serve
with a long straw.

LONG ISLAND ICED TEA
Highball glass

INGREDIENTS
I oz. vodka
I oz. gin
I oz. light rum
I oz. tequila
I oz. lemon juice
I oz. orange liqueur
I tsp. superfine sugar
3 oz. cola
slice of lemon and lime to garnish

METHOD
Pour all ingredients into a highball
glass full of ice and stir. Garnish with
half a slice of lemon and half a slice of
lime, and serve with a swizzle stick and
two tall straws.

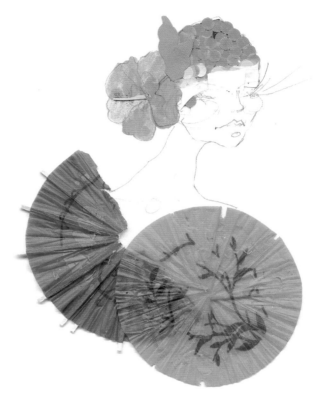

HIBISCUS MARTINI
Martini glass

INGREDIENTS
1½ oz. vodka
½ oz. blackberry liqueur
½ oz. cranberry juice
½ oz. apple juice
2 tsp. hibiscus cordial
dash of lemon juice
cranberry to garnish

METHOD
Shake all ingredients and strain
into a martini glass. Garnish with
a speared cranberry.

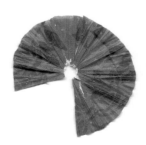

HAWAIIAN PIMMS

Pilsner glass

INGREDIENTS

½ lemon, cut into wedges
5 mint leaves
I tsp. sugar syrup
I½ oz. Pimms
I½ oz. vodka
splash of ginger ale

METHOD

Muddle lemon, mint and sugar.
Combine with ice, Pimms and vodka,
and shake. Serve in a Pilsner glass and
top with ginger ale.

ORANGE & PEACH SWIZZLE

Martini glass

INGREDIENTS

I oz. vodka
½ oz. peach liqueur
½ oz. lemon juice
I oz. passionfruit puree
3–4 dashes of orange bitters
slice of peach, vanilla sugar and
**   passionfruit pulp to garnish**

METHOD

Shake all ingredients and serve straight
up in a chilled martini glass. Garnish
with a speared peach slice and a pinch
of vanilla sugar and drizzle passionfruit
pulp at the bottom of the glass.

VELVET UNDERGROUND
Martini glass

INGREDIENTS
1½ oz. honey-infused vodka
½ oz. apple liqueur
3 tbsp. apple sauce
2 tsp. lemon juice
2 drops of balsamic vinegar
slice of apple to garnish

METHOD
Shake vodka, liqueur, sauce and juice with ice, then double-strain into a martini glass. Drop balsamic vinegar in the center of the glass and garnish with a round slice of apple.

VANILLA PASSION
Martini glass

INGREDIENTS
1½ oz. vanilla-infused vodka
½ oz. apple juice
1 oz. passionfruit puree
½ oz. caramel liqueur
2–3 dashes of lime
splash of vanilla sugar syrup
**passionfruit pulp and vanilla bean
   to garnish**

METHOD
Shake all ingredients and serve straight up in a chilled martini glass. Garnish with passionfruit pulp and a split vanilla bean.

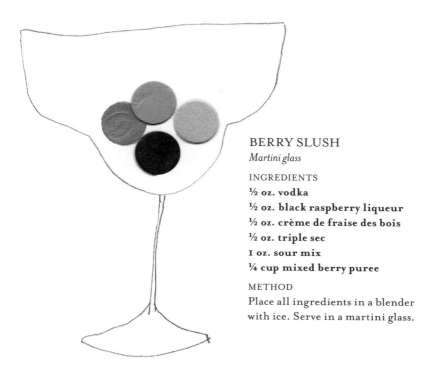

BERRY SLUSH
Martini glass

INGREDIENTS
½ oz. vodka
½ oz. black raspberry liqueur
½ oz. crème de fraise des bois
½ oz. triple sec
I oz. sour mix
¼ cup mixed berry puree

METHOD
Place all ingredients in a blender
with ice. Serve in a martini glass.

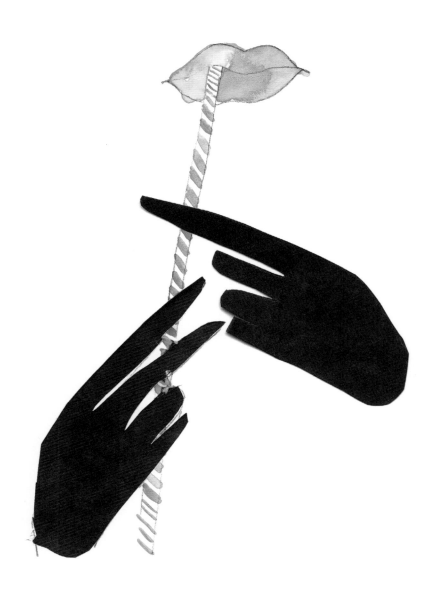

BLOOD ORANGE
BITTER HAND
Martini glass

INGREDIENTS
1½ oz. vodka
½ oz. Cointreau
1 oz. blood orange juice
dash of orange bitters
orange zest to garnish

METHOD
Shake and strain all ingredients into
a martini glass. Garnish with flamed
orange zest.

BUSH TUCKERMAN'S
SINUS CLEANER
Martini glass

INGREDIENTS
1 oz. tamarind-infused vodka
½ oz. vodka
½ oz. Jaggard lemon myrtle
2 tsp. honey liqueur
½ oz. lemon juice
2 tsp. ginger syrup
2 oz. mineral water
1 tsp. honey
slice of lemon to garnish

METHOD
Shake all ingredients with ice and
strain into a chilled martini glass.
Garnish with a lemon slice.

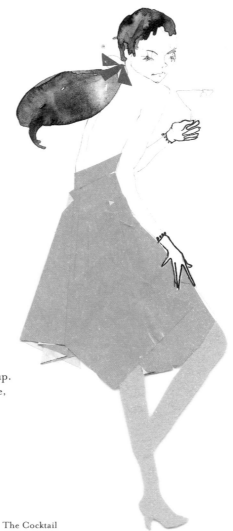

BASIL BOO
Martini glass

INGREDIENTS
6 fresh basil leaves
2 wedges of lime
2 tsp. coconut syrup
I oz. orange-infused vodka
I oz. pineapple-infused vodka
2 tbsp. fresh pineapple pulp
I oz. pineapple juice

METHOD
Muddle basil, lime and coconut syrup.
Shake with other ingredients and ice,
and strain into a martini glass.

CITRUS LIME GIMLET
Martini glass

INGREDIENTS
3 oz. citrus-infused vodka
1½ oz. lime juice
1½ oz. sugar syrup
slice of lime to garnish

METHOD
Shake all ingredients with ice
and strain into a martini glass.
Garnish with a lime slice.

ELDERTINI
Martini glass

INGREDIENTS
1½ oz. vodka
2 tsp. Cinzano Bianco
½ oz. orange elderflower cordial
twist of lemon to garnish

METHOD
Shake and strain all ingredients
into a martini glass. Garnish with
a lemon twist.

RED DEATH

Old-fashioned glass

INGREDIENTS

1 oz. vodka
1 oz. Southern Comfort
1 oz. amaretto
½ oz. sloe gin
½ oz. triple sec
dash of lime juice
splash of orange juice

METHOD

Pour all ingredients (except orange juice) over ice in an old-fashioned glass. Fill with orange juice.

KRACKED

Highball glass

INGREDIENTS

2 strawberries
2 tsp. lemon juice
1½ oz. vanilla-infused vodka
2 tsp. crème de cassis
2 tsp. crème de fraise
1 oz. Twinings red fruits tea
cracked pepper to garnish

METHOD

Muddle strawberries and lemon juice. Shake with remaining ingredients and ice, and strain into a highball glass over ice cubes. Open the strainer to release some fruit for texture, then top with crushed ice. Garnish with cracked pepper and serve with a long straw.

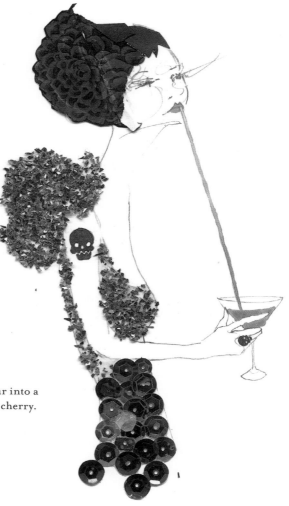

PAUL'S POISON
Martini glass

INGREDIENTS
1 oz. vanilla-infused vodka
1 oz. lemon juice
1 oz. apple liqueur
dash of sugar syrup
cherry to garnish

METHOD
Shake all ingredients and pour into a
martini glass. Garnish with a cherry.

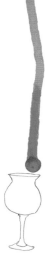

SCREWDRIVER
Highball glass

INGREDIENTS
½ oz. vodka
2 oz. orange juice
slice of orange to garnish

METHOD
Pour vodka and orange juice over ice
in a highball glass. Cut orange slice
in half and sit both pieces on the rim
of the glass.

KAMIKAZE
Tumbler

INGREDIENTS
I oz. vodka
I oz. triple sec
I oz. lime juice

METHOD
Shake ingredients with ice and strain
into a tumbler.

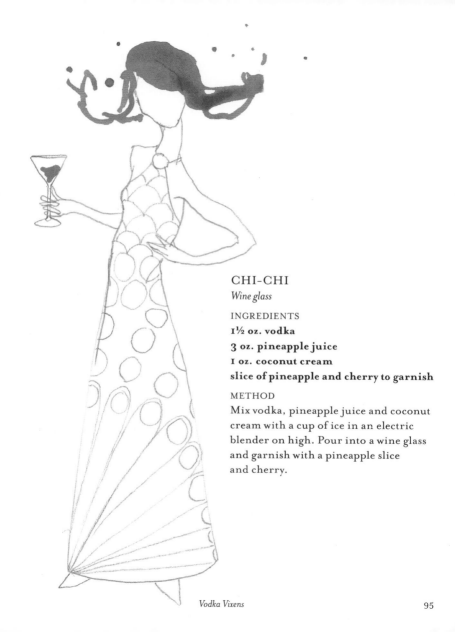

CHI-CHI
Wine glass

INGREDIENTS
1½ oz. vodka
3 oz. pineapple juice
1 oz. coconut cream
slice of pineapple and cherry to garnish

METHOD
Mix vodka, pineapple juice and coconut cream with a cup of ice in an electric blender on high. Pour into a wine glass and garnish with a pineapple slice and cherry.

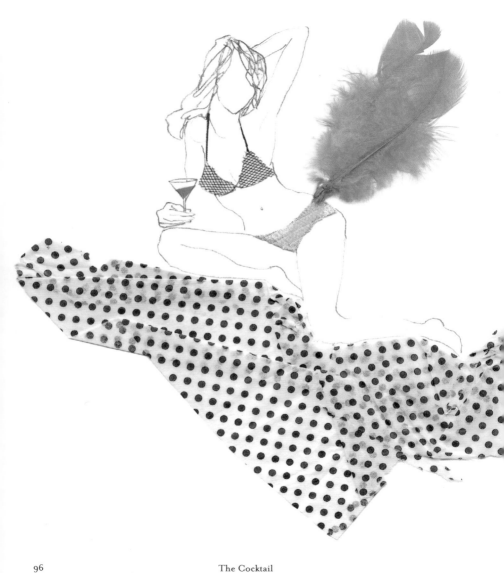

The Cocktail

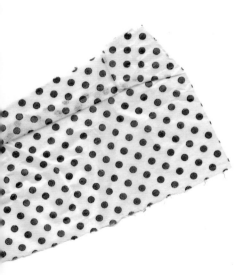

SEX ON THE BEACH
Highball glass

INGREDIENTS
1 oz. vodka
1½ oz. peach schnapps
2 oz. cranberry juice
2 oz. grapefruit juice
wedge of lime to garnish

METHOD
Shake all the ingredients with ice
and strain into a highball glass.
Garnish with a lime wedge.

WHITE RUSSIAN
Old-fashioned glass

INGREDIENTS
I oz. vodka
I oz. light cream
I oz. Kahlúa

METHOD
Shake all the ingredients with ice and
strain into an old-fashioned glass over
ice cubes.

CONFUCIUS
Martini glass

INGREDIENTS
6 canned lychees
4 chunks of fresh ginger
½ oz. fresh lemon juice
I tsp. lychee syrup
I½ oz. lemongrass-infused vodka
½ oz. sake
extra lychee to garnish

METHOD
Muddle lychees with ginger. Add juice,
syrup and alcohol. Shake on ice and
double-strain into a martini glass.
Garnish with a skewered lychee.

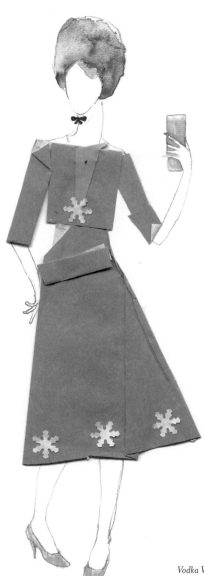

GODMOTHER
Highball glass

INGREDIENTS
2 oz. vodka
1 oz. amaretto

METHOD
Stir both ingredients in a mixing glass
with ice and strain into a highball glass.

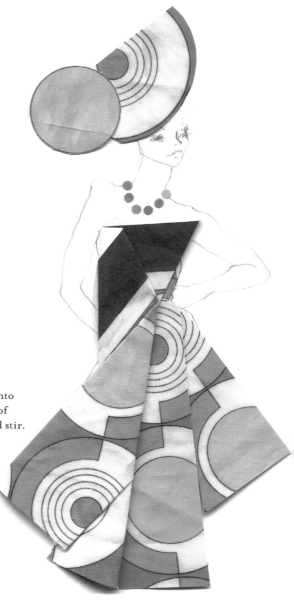

RETROINFUSION
Martini glass

INGREDIENTS
1 oz. strawberry-infused vodka
1 oz. vanilla-infused vodka
1 oz. passionfruit liqueur
1 passionfruit

METHOD
Shake alcohol with ice and strain into
a chilled martini glass. Pour pulp of
whole passionfruit over the top and stir.

MOULIN ROUGE
Tumbler

INGREDIENTS
10 raspberries
1 lemon
1 oz. honey-infused vodka
½ oz. black raspberry liqueur
½ oz. macadamia nut liqueur
mint leaf to garnish

METHOD
Muddle fresh raspberries and lemon.
Combine with alcohol, shake and serve
with crushed ice. Garnish with mint.

FARRANG
Tumbler

INGREDIENTS
½ lime
1 tsp. sugar
5 cilantro leaves
1 oz. chili-infused vodka
**½ oz. crème de gingembre
    or other ginger liqueur**

METHOD
Muddle lime, sugar and cilantro and
combine with crushed ice in a tumbler.
Top with vodka and crème de gingembre.
Stir and serve.

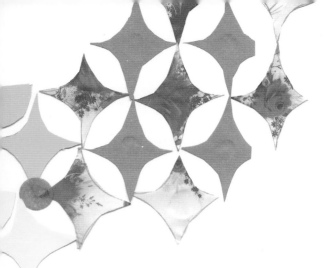

ROSE & ORANGE BLOSSOM MARTINI

Martini glass

INGREDIENTS

1½ oz. rose petal–infused vodka
½ oz. Cointreau
1 tsp. Campari
1 oz. pink grapefruit juice
3 drops of orange bitters
2 tsp. sugar syrup
orange zest to garnish

METHOD

Pour all ingredients into a mixing glass
with ice. Shake and double-strain into
a martini glass. Garnish with burnt
orange zest.

CITRUS FINISH

Martini glass

INGREDIENTS

1½ oz. citrus-infused vodka
1 oz. Cointreau
splash of Champagne
1 lemon
twist of lemon and orange to garnish

METHOD

Shake vodka and Cointreau and strain
into a martini glass. Top with Champagne
and a squeeze of lemon. Garnish with
twists of lemon and orange.

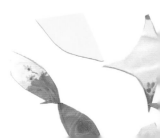

The Cocktail

CAMPRINHA
Highball glass

INGREDIENTS

1 lime, cut into wedges
1 tsp. sugar
½ oz. vodka
1 oz. Campari
½ oz. lime liqueur
wedge of lemon to garnish

METHOD

Muddle lime and sugar. Combine with alcohol and serve on ice. Garnish with a lemon wedge.

CAIPIROSKA
Tumbler

INGREDIENTS

2 limes, cut into wedges
½ tsp. sugar
2 oz. vodka

METHOD

Muddle lime and sugar at the bottom of a tumbler. Cover with crushed ice and top with vodka.

VALENTINE
Martini glass

INGREDIENTS
1½ oz. flower-infused vodka
2 tsp. black raspberry liqueur
pomegranate molasses to garnish

METHOD
Pour vodka and liqueur into a blender.
Mix well and serve immediately in a
molasses-rimmed martini glass.

MISTY BITCH
Highball glass

INGREDIENTS
1 oz. vodka
1 oz. Campari
1 lime
splash of pink grapefruit juice

METHOD
Mix vodka and Campari in a highball
glass. Add fresh lime to taste and top
with pink grapefruit juice.

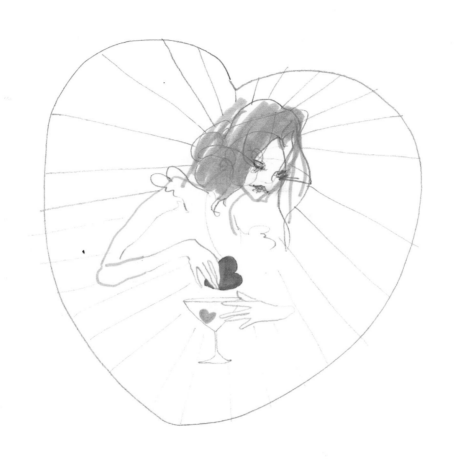

CHOCOLATE MARTINI

Martini glass

INGREDIENTS

3 chocolate morsels
cocoa to garnish
1 oz. vodka
1 oz. white crème de cacao

METHOD

Place chocolate morsels in the bottom of
a martini glass and dust rim with cocoa.
Shake vodka and crème de cacao with
ice, and strain into a martini glass.

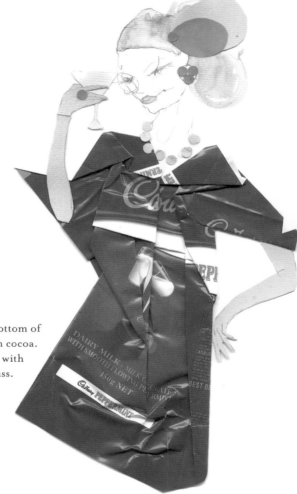

PURPLE HAZE

Champagne flute

INGREDIENTS

3 basil leaves
3 lychees
1 tsp. lemon juice
½ oz. white grapefruit juice
1½ oz. vodka
2 tsp. sugar syrup
1 tsp. elderflower cordial
purple basil leaf to garnish

METHOD

Muddle basil, lychees, lemon juice and
grapefruit juice, then add remaining
ingredients and ice. Shake and double-
strain into a flute. Float a purple basil
leaf to garnish.

HAPPY MEDIUM

Martini glass

INGREDIENTS

1 oz. spiced rum
1 oz. chocolate-infused vodka
1 tsp. cinnamon syrup
cinnamon stick to garnish

METHOD

Stir all ingredients and serve in a martini
glass. Garnish with a cinnamon stick.

APHRODITE
Martini glass

INGREDIENTS
1 oz. orange-infused vodka
1½ oz. peach-infused vodka
1 oz. grenadine
1 oz. lemon juice
1 oz. raspberry puree

METHOD
Shake all ingredients with ice
and strain into a martini glass.

AFTER SEX
Collins glass

INGREDIENTS
1½ oz. vodka
2 tsp. crème de banane
splash of orange juice

METHOD
Pour vodka and crème de banane
over ice in a Collins glass and fill
with orange juice.

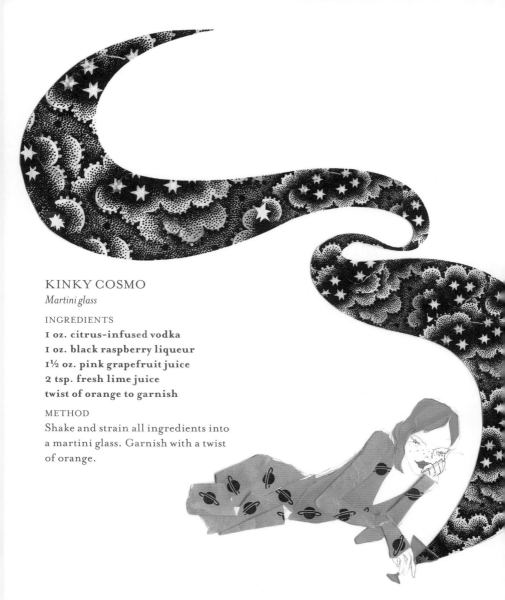

KINKY COSMO
Martini glass

INGREDIENTS
1 oz. citrus-infused vodka
1 oz. black raspberry liqueur
1½ oz. pink grapefruit juice
2 tsp. fresh lime juice
twist of orange to garnish

METHOD
Shake and strain all ingredients into
a martini glass. Garnish with a twist
of orange.

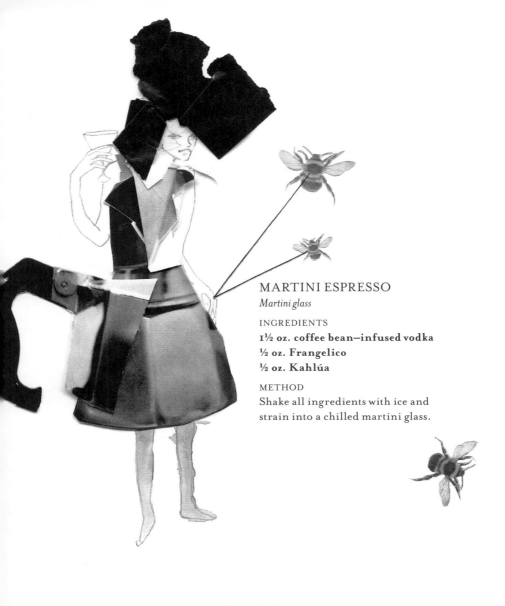

MARTINI ESPRESSO
Martini glass

INGREDIENTS
1½ oz. coffee bean—infused vodka
½ oz. Frangelico
½ oz. Kahlúa

METHOD
Shake all ingredients with ice and
strain into a chilled martini glass.

HONEY ESPRESSO

Martini glass

INGREDIENTS
I oz. vodka
I oz. honey-infused vodka
I tsp. sugar syrup
I oz. espresso shot
coffee beans to garnish

METHOD
Shake all ingredients and double-strain into a martini glass. Garnish with three coffee beans.

MUDSLIDE

Highball glass

INGREDIENTS
2 oz. vodka
2 oz. Kahlúa
2 oz. Irish cream

METHOD
Shake all ingredients with crushed ice. Serve in a chilled highball glass.

HEAD CLEANER
Martini glass

INGREDIENTS
1½ oz. vodka
1 oz. lemon juice
2 tsp. ginger wine
dash of sugar syrup
candied ginger to garnish

METHOD
Shake all ingredients and pour into a martini glass. Garnish with a piece of candied ginger.

TIBETAN MULE
Highball glass

INGREDIENTS
4 chunks of pineapple
5 cilantro stems with leaves
2 tsp. lime juice
1 oz. pineapple-infused vodka
½ oz. sake
½ oz. crème de gingembre
2 tsp. sugar syrup
1½ oz. ginger ale
cilantro leaf to garnish

METHOD
Muddle pineapple, cilantro stems and lime juice. Combine with vodka, sake, crème de gingembre, sugar syrup and ice, and shake. Pour into a highball glass, opening the strainer to release some fruit for texture, and top with ginger ale. Garnish with a cilantro leaf.

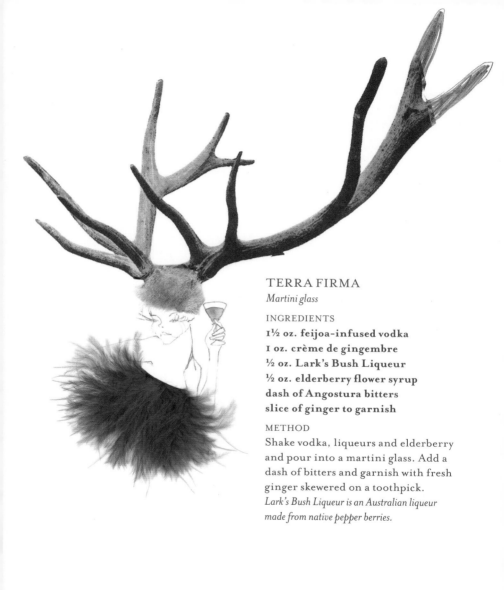

TERRA FIRMA
Martini glass

INGREDIENTS
1½ oz. feijoa-infused vodka
1 oz. crème de gingembre
½ oz. Lark's Bush Liqueur
½ oz. elderberry flower syrup
dash of Angostura bitters
slice of ginger to garnish

METHOD
Shake vodka, liqueurs and elderberry
and pour into a martini glass. Add a
dash of bitters and garnish with fresh
ginger skewered on a toothpick.
Lark's Bush Liqueur is an Australian liqueur
made from native pepper berries.

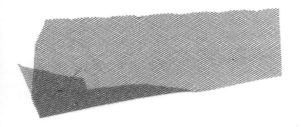

going against the grain

Whiskey and its white trash cousin, bourbon, are no longer just a guy's best friend. There are plenty of modern women who don't mind the hearty drop, and the rush of grainy cocktails being served in bars is 100% distilled proof.

There's an outlaw's bravado associated with bourbon. It's biker tough and —like old-school bikers—it sometimes smells as if it hasn't bathed in months. But before you write off bourbon or whiskey as being too low-frill or groupie for your Jimmy Choo shoes, take a swig and reappraise.

These drinks are primal and, honey, they're not low carb. They're Real Drinks for Real Babes who think that Atkins died because he didn't have enough bourbon in his diet. For a classic drop, try the Manhattan or Rusty Nail. For something edgy and new, chirp like a Kentucky Bluebird or dig your heels in with a Stiletto. These dark drops are for devoted dames who don't give a damn, Miss Scarlett.

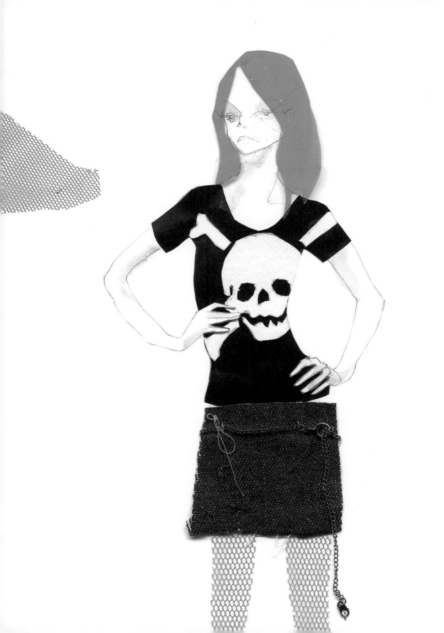

BRITISH RAJ
Old-fashioned glass

INGREDIENTS
¼ pear
2 oz. single malt whiskey
½ oz. star anise sugar syrup
1 oz. lime juice
slices of pear and lime to garnish

METHOD
Muddle pear, then shake with whiskey,
syrup and juice. Strain into an
old-fashioned glass over crushed ice.
Garnish with a slice of pear and lime.

GENTLEMAN'S AGREEMENT
Martini glass

INGREDIENTS
2 oz. bourbon
½ oz. Grand Marnier
2 tsp. caramel syrup
raisins to garnish

METHOD
Pour ingredients into a martini glass,
stir and serve. Garnish with raisins
steeped in bourbon.

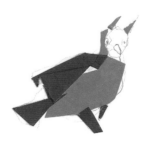

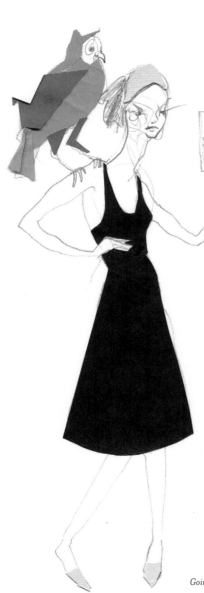

KENTUCKY BLUEBIRD
Martini glass

INGREDIENTS
8 blueberries
2 tsp. caramel syrup
1 oz. bourbon
2 tsp. barrel-proof bourbon
½ oz. blueberry liqueur
½ oz. vanilla liqueur
2 tsp. cabernet sauvignon
2 tsp. lemon juice
½ oz. unfiltered apple juice
4 blueberries to garnish

METHOD
Muddle blueberries and caramel syrup.
Combine with other ingredients and ice,
then shake and strain into a chilled martini
glass. Garnish with four blueberries, either
on a skewer or floating across the top.

WHISKEY DATE SOUR

Old-fashioned glass

INGREDIENTS

1½ oz. date-infused whiskey
1½ oz. lemon juice
2 tsp. egg white
dash of Angostura bitters

METHOD

Shake all ingredients and strain into an old-fashioned glass.

WHISKEY MULE

Highball glass

INGREDIENTS

2 oz. whiskey
1 oz. lime juice
2 tsp. sugar syrup
splash of ginger ale
sprig of mint to garnish

METHOD

Shake and strain whiskey, juice and syrup into a highball glass. Top with ginger ale and garnish with a mint sprig.

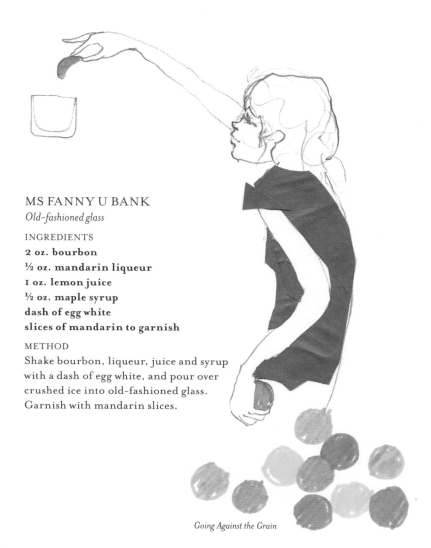

MS FANNY U BANK
Old-fashioned glass

INGREDIENTS

2 oz. bourbon
½ oz. mandarin liqueur
1 oz. lemon juice
½ oz. maple syrup
dash of egg white
slices of mandarin to garnish

METHOD
Shake bourbon, liqueur, juice and syrup
with a dash of egg white, and pour over
crushed ice into old-fashioned glass.
Garnish with mandarin slices.

STILETTO

Old-fashioned glass

INGREDIENTS

1½ oz. bourbon
1½ tsp. amaretto
juice of ½ lemon

METHOD

Pour all ingredients into an
old-fashioned glass over ice and stir.

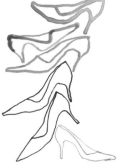

RUSTY NAIL

Old-fashioned glass

INGREDIENTS

1 oz. scotch whiskey
1½ oz. Drambuie

METHOD

Pour whiskey and Drambuie into an
old-fashioned glass, with ice.

IRISH CAR BOMB
Pilsner glass/Shot glass

INGREDIENTS
½ oz. Baileys Irish Cream
½ oz. Irish whiskey
14 oz. Guinness Stout

METHOD
Pour Baileys into a shot glass and layer
whiskey on top. Pour Guinness into a
Pilsner glass and let settle. Drop the shot
glass into the Guinness and chug. If you
don't drink this quickly, it will curdle
and taste horrible.

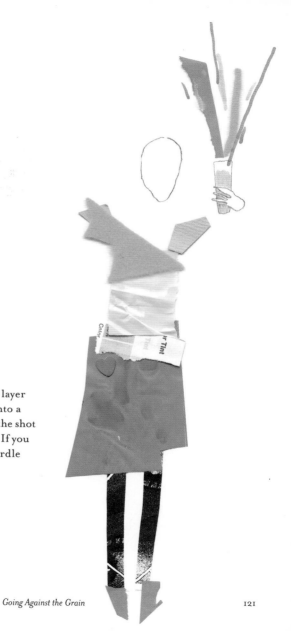

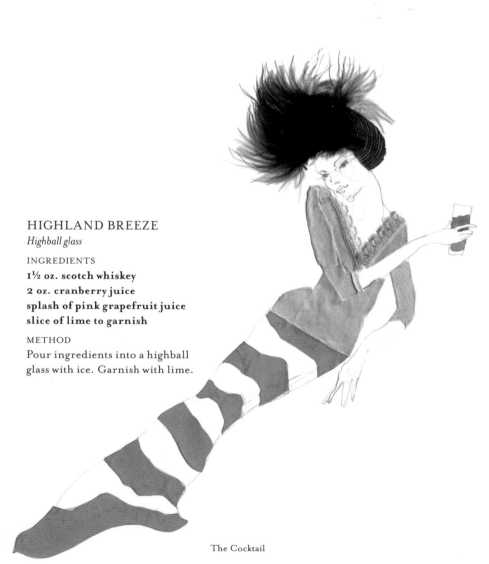

HIGHLAND BREEZE
Highball glass

INGREDIENTS
1½ oz. scotch whiskey
2 oz. cranberry juice
splash of pink grapefruit juice
slice of lime to garnish

METHOD
Pour ingredients into a highball
glass with ice. Garnish with lime.

SIT BACK AND RELAX
Highball glass

INGREDIENTS
3–4 slices of lime
4–5 mint leaves
1 tsp. brown sugar
2 oz. scotch whiskey
½ oz. Grand Marnier
sprig of mint to garnish

METHOD
Muddle limes, mint and sugar at the
base of a highball glass. Build whiskey
and Grand Marnier on top. Garnish
with a mint sprig.

BOURBON STONE MARTINI
Martini glass

INGREDIENTS
1½ oz. bourbon
1 oz. orange curacao
1 oz. fresh lemon juice
1 oz. orange juice
1 tsp. superfine sugar

METHOD
Shake all ingredients with ice and
strain into a martini glass.

MANHATTAN

Martini glass

INGREDIENTS

2½ oz. bourbon
½ oz. sweet vermouth
4 dashes of Angostura bitters
maraschino cherry
orange peel to garnish

METHOD

Combine bourbon, vermouth and bitters
in a mixing glass with ice. Strain over a
cherry placed in a chilled martini glass.
Rub the cut edge of the orange peel over
the glass rim and twist it over the drink.

PAUL'S MANHATTAN

Highball glass

INGREDIENTS

2½ oz. scotch whiskey
2 tsp. Dubonnet Red
2 tsp. extra-dry vermouth
dash of Angostura bitters
2 tsp. of maraschino juice
cherry and twist of lemon to garnish

METHOD

Combine all ingredients and stir well.
Strain over ice in a highball glass.
Garnish with a cherry and lemon twist.

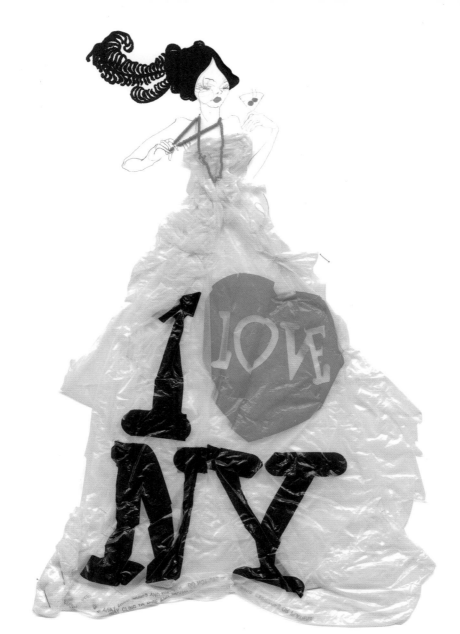

OLD-FASHIONED
WHISKEY SOUR
Martini glass

INGREDIENTS
1½ oz. whiskey
2 dashes of Angostura bitters
4 tsp. cherry juice
5 oz. sweet and sour mix
olives or mushrooms to garnish

METHOD
Mix whiskey, bitters and cherry juice in
an ice-filled martini glass, and fill the
remainder of the glass with sour mix.
Garnish with olives or mushrooms and
serve with a swizzle stick.

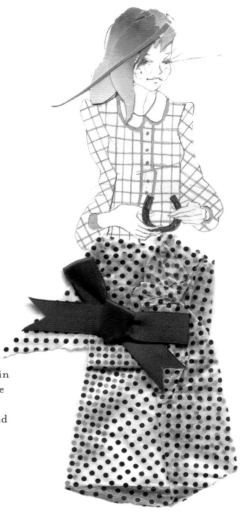

The Cocktail

OLD-FASHIONED

Old-fashioned glass

INGREDIENTS

I tsp. sugar
splash of water
2 dashes of Angostura bitters
I maraschino cherry
wedge of orange
2 oz. bourbon

METHOD

Mix sugar, water and bitters in an
old-fashioned glass. Add cherry and
orange wedge. Muddle into a paste,
then add bourbon. Fill with ice and stir.

BOURBON MILK PUNCH

Old-fashioned glass

INGREDIENTS

2 oz. bourbon
3 oz. half and half
I tsp. superfine sugar
¼ tsp. vanilla extract
¼ tsp. grated nutmeg to garnish

METHOD

Shake all the ingredients with ice cubes
and strain into an old-fashioned glass.
Garnish with nutmeg on top.

GODFATHER

Old-fashioned glass

INGREDIENTS

I oz. bourbon
I oz. amaretto
2 wedges of lime to garnish

METHOD
Build bourbon and amaretto in
an ice-filled old-fashioned glass.
Top with lime wedges.

BOURBON COLLINS

Collins glass

INGREDIENTS

2 oz. bourbon
I oz. fresh lemon juice
I oz. sugar syrup
splash of soda water
cherry and slice of orange to garnish

METHOD
Fill two-thirds of a Collins glass
with ice and pour ingredients over it.
Garnish with a cherry and a slice
of orange.

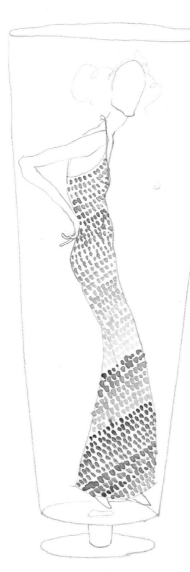

BOSTON SOUR
Whiskey sour glass

INGREDIENTS
2 oz. whiskey
juice of ½ lemon
I tsp. superfine sugar
I egg white
2 dashes of Angostura bitters
slice of lemon
cherry to garnish

METHOD
Shake whiskey, lemon juice, sugar and
egg white with ice and slice of lemon
into a whiskey sour glass, top with the
cherry and serve.

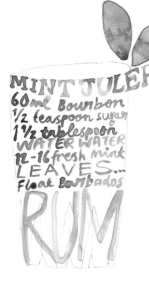

MINT JULEP
Old-fashioned glass

INGREDIENTS
I tsp. superfine sugar
5–6 mint leaves
3 oz. bourbon
sprig of mint to garnish

METHOD
Muddle mint leaves with superfine sugar
and a splash of water in an old-fashioned
glass. Fill with ice, top with bourbon
and garnish with mint sprig.

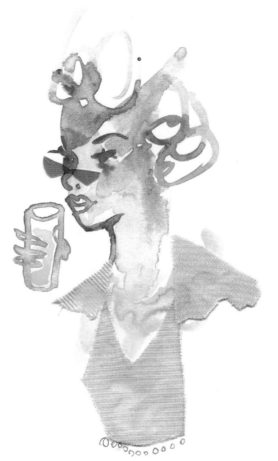

AMERICAN SWEETHEART
Tumbler

INGREDIENTS
1 oz. bourbon
1 oz. Southern Comfort
dash of dry vermouth
splash of sweet and sour mix

METHOD
Shake all ingredients with ice
and pour into a tumbler.

SOUTHERN SHAG

Highball glass

INGREDIENTS

1½ oz. Southern Comfort
2 oz. cranberry juice
½ oz. orange juice
wedge of lime to garnish

METHOD

Fill a highball glass with ice, add
Southern Comfort and cranberry
and orange juices, then stir.
Garnish with a lime wedge.

SWIZZLE

Highball glass

INGREDIENTS

5 chunks of pineapple
½ orange, peeled and quartered
1 tsp. vanilla sugar
4 dashes of Angostura bitters
1½ oz. bourbon
2 tsp. lemon juice
dash of Grand Marnier
sprig of mint to garnish

METHOD

Muddle fruit, sugar and bitters.
Add bourbon. Fill ½ a highball glass
with crushed ice. Stir and top with
fresh ice. Float Grand Marnier on
top and garnish with a mint sprig.

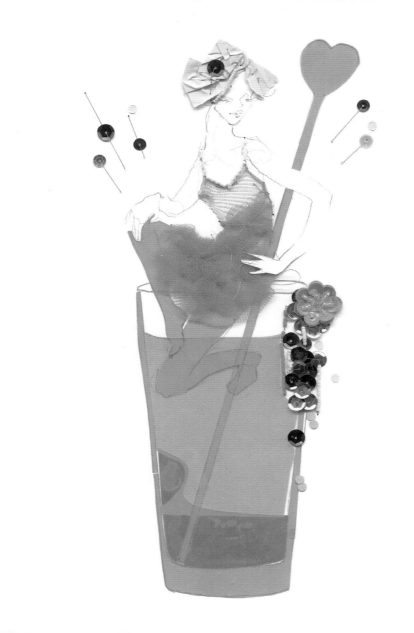

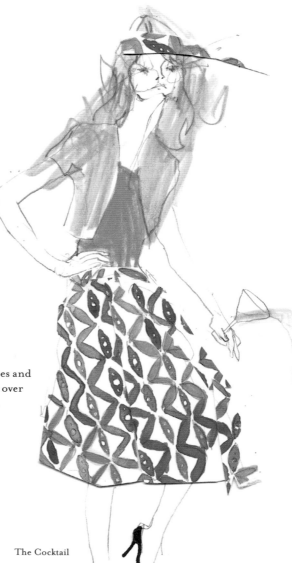

LOUISVILLE COOLER
Old-fashioned glass

INGREDIENTS
2 oz. bourbon
I oz. orange juice
½ oz. lime juice
I tsp. superfine sugar
slice of orange to garnish

METHOD
Shake all ingredients with ice cubes and
strain into an old-fashioned glass over
ice. Garnish with an orange slice.

ALABAMA SLAMMER

Highball glass

INGREDIENTS

1 oz. Southern Comfort
½ oz. sloe gin
½ oz. amaretto
splash of orange juice
slice of orange to garnish

METHOD

Fill a highball glass with ice, add
ingredients and stir. Garnish with
orange slice.

SOCRATES

Martini glass

INGREDIENTS

2 oz. scotch whiskey
1 oz. apricot brandy
1 tsp. triple sec
dash of Angostura bitters

METHOD

Combine all ingredients in a mixing
glass with ice, stir and strain into a
martini glass.

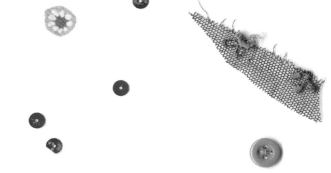

for the mixed-up gal

We've all been lost and jaded in life, walked the path less followed and failed in our attempts. We knew the path we chose meant trouble, but we went along for the ride anyway. It's on nights like these that you need to take a leaf out of this chapter. Round up your drinking buddies to sweep up the mess (by getting mischievously messy all over again).

The mixed-up gal is a unique fashionista—she mixes the new with a touch of the vintage, teams faux pas stoles with well-worn jeans, pleated skirts with fishnet stockings and fitted boots, ruffled shirts with a tight second-hand sweater. She doesn't follow fashion rules dictated by the glossies—she's a find in her own right and takes the best of what she stumbles across.

This chapter is for girls who can't decide on a signature drink, but want to get the best of all worlds. When you do slip up, consider a Freudian Slip or, for something more cheeky, there's Beneath the Sheets for some hotted-up fun. Whatever your plight in life, the mixed-up gal is sure to keep things interesting (to say the least).

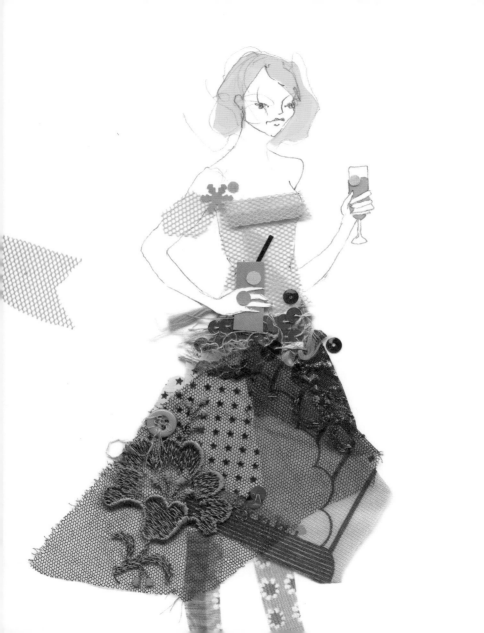

KENTUCKY APPLE
Highball glass

INGREDIENTS

2—3 chunks of apple
½ oz. elderflower cordial
1½ oz. bourbon
½ oz. green apple liqueur
1½ oz. apple juice
wedge of apple to garnish

METHOD

Muddle apple and elderflower cordial.
Shake with remaining ingredients.
Strain over ice—½ cubed, ½ crushed
—into a highball glass. Garnish with a
speared apple wedge.

SPRITZER

Highball glass

INGREDIENTS

3 oz. white wine
2 oz. soda water
slice of lemon or orange to garnish

METHOD

Fill a highball glass with ice, then fill
three-quarters with wine and the
remainder with soda water. Garnish
with a twist of lemon or orange.

KARMA SIP TRA

Old-fashioned glass

INGREDIENTS

2 lime chunks
6 seedless red grapes
6 mint leaves
I oz. Bacardi Limon
½ oz. Cinzano Bianco
2 tsp. blackberry liqueur
I oz. apple juice
dash of soda water
sprig of mint to garnish

METHOD

Muddle fruit with mint. Combine with
alcohol, juice and ice. Shake and pour
into an old-fashioned glass. Top with
soda water and crushed ice. Garnish with
a sprig of mint.

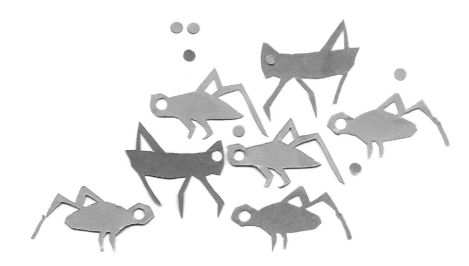

OPIUM
Old-fashioned glass

INGREDIENTS
10 blueberries
6 blackberries
2 strawberries
½ oz. sugar syrup
4 mint leaves
1 oz. white rum
½ oz. lemon liqueur
½ oz. black raspberry liqueur
2 tsp. ginger liqueur
1½ oz. cranberry juice
ginger to garnish

METHOD
Muddle fruit, sugar syrup and mint,
and shake with other ingredients into
an old-fashioned glass. Garnish with
finely chopped ginger.

GRASSHOPPER
Martini glass

INGREDIENTS
1 oz. crème de menthe
1 oz. white crème de cacao
1 oz. light cream

METHOD
Shake all ingredients with ice.
Strain into a martini glass and serve.

YANG TAO

Martini glass

INGREDIENTS
½ kiwi fruit
1 oz. Cointreau
½ oz. crème de fraise
½ oz. white rum
1 oz. guava juice
strawberry to garnish

METHOD
Muddle kiwi fruit, and shake with other ingredients. Strain into a martini glass and garnish with a strawberry.

SDP

Martini glass

INGREDIENTS
1 oz. Jaggard original
½ oz. Licor 43
½ oz. butterscotch schnapps
1 tsp. heavy cream
strawberry to garnish

METHOD
Shake all ingredients and double-strain into a martini glass. Garnish with a strawberry.
Jaggard original is a fruit liqueur made from the native Australian quandong fruit.

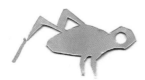

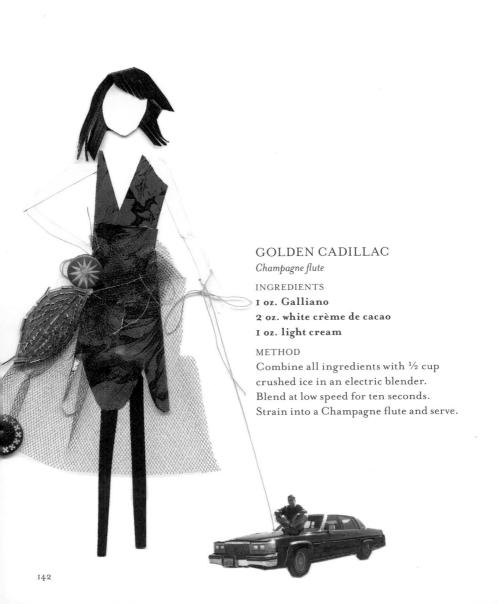

GOLDEN CADILLAC

Champagne flute

INGREDIENTS

1 oz. Galliano
2 oz. white crème de cacao
1 oz. light cream

METHOD

Combine all ingredients with ½ cup
crushed ice in an electric blender.
Blend at low speed for ten seconds.
Strain into a Champagne flute and serve.

BRANDY ALEXANDER
Champagne flute

INGREDIENTS
1 oz. dark crème de cacao
1 oz. brandy
splash of cream
ground nutmeg to garnish

METHOD
Combine ingredients with ice and
blend. Strain into a Champagne flute
and garnish with a sprinkle of nutmeg.

GIUSEPPE HABIT
Martini glass

INGREDIENTS
twist of lemon
1½ oz. Galliano
½ oz. Frangelico
1 oz. Cointreau
2 oz. apple juice
2 twists of lemon to garnish

METHOD
Twist lemon into shaker, combine with
other ingredients and shake. Strain into
a martini glass and garnish with twists
of lemon.

LOUISIANA SLING
Highball glass

INGREDIENTS
1½ oz. Herbsaint
1 oz. lemon juice
½ oz. sugar syrup
½ oz. Cointreau
2 oz. pineapple juice
wedge of lemon to garnish

METHOD
Shake and strain all ingredients
into a highball glass with crushed ice.
Garnish with a wedge of lemon.

BELLINI COCKTAIL
Champagne flute

INGREDIENTS
1 oz. peach nectar
½ tsp. lemon juice
1 oz. peach schnapps
1½ oz. Champagne

METHOD
Mix the peach nectar, lemon juice and
schnapps in a chilled flute. Add crushed
ice, stir, and add Champagne.

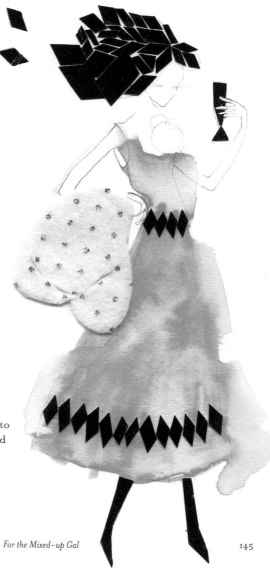

COUTURE FIZZ
Champagne flute

INGREDIENTS
1 tsp. Campari
2 tsp. black raspberry liqueur
2 strawberries or raspberries
dash of lemon juice
dash of sugar syrup
4½ oz. Champagne
slice of strawberry to garnish

METHOD
Combine all ingredients (except
Champagne) in a mixing glass.
Chill, shake and double-strain into
a flute. Layer with Champagne and
float a strawberry slice.

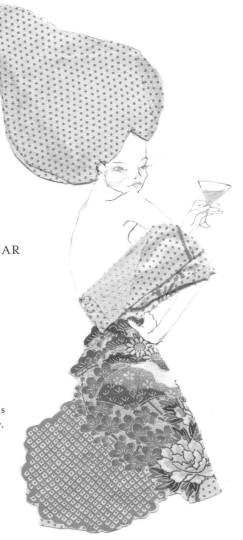

PEAR & CARDAMON SIDECAR
Martini glass

INGREDIENTS
7 pods of green cardamon
1 oz. Cointreau
½ oz. pear liqueur
1 oz. lemon juice
1 oz. cognac
slice of pear to garnish

METHOD
Break away shells of cardamon pods
and muddle seeds in base of shaker.
Add all ingredients, shake and
double-strain into a martini glass.
Garnish with a fanned pear slice.

NAPOLI ICED TEA
Pilsner glass

INGREDIENTS
2 chunks of lemon
5 chunks of orange
1 oz. vanilla-infused Rosso
½ oz. Cointreau
2 tsp. vanilla liqueur
1 oz. orange juice
1 oz. Twinings red fruits tea
2 tsp. sugar syrup
slices of orange and lemon to garnish

METHOD
Muddle fruit and combine with other
ingredients. Shake and strain into
a pilsner glass. Garnish with orange
and lemon slices.

BANGKOK ICED TEA
Highball glass

INGREDIENTS
3 leaves of Italian basil
3 wedges of lime
6 mint leaves
2 tsp. dry vermouth
1½ basil-infused Cinzano Bianco
splash of lemon and ginger tea
splash of ginger ale

METHOD
Muddle basil and lime. Add mint, alcohol
and ice, then shake. Pour into a highball
glass. Top with lemon and ginger tea
(cold) and ginger ale.

FRENCH PASSION
Old-fashioned glass

INGREDIENTS
1½ oz. cognac
1 oz. vanilla liqueur
½ oz. passionfruit liqueur
1 oz. lemon juice
dash of vanilla extract
1 passionfruit to garnish
slice of lemon to garnish

METHOD
Shake and strain all ingredients into
an old-fashioned glass. Garnish with
passionfruit pulp and a lemon slice.

AFFOGATO—FRENCH STYLE
Old-fashioned glass

INGREDIENTS
2 scoops of vanilla ice cream
1 oz. Cointreau
1 oz. cognac
1 espresso shot

METHOD
Spoon the ice cream into a large
old-fashioned glass. Top with alcohol
and finish with a shot of espresso.
Serve with a teaspoon.

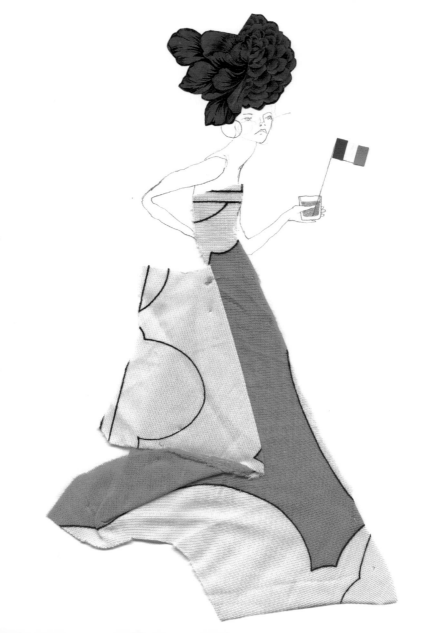

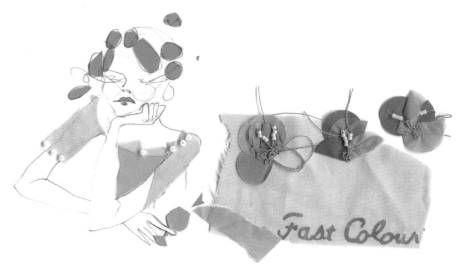

RINKY DINK SPECIAL
Martini glass

INGREDIENTS
**I oz. apricot brandy
I oz. fresh lemon juice
2 tsp. Cointreau
2 tsp. Galliano
dash of sugar syrup
twist of orange to garnish**

METHOD
Shake all ingredients and pour
into a martini glass. Garnish with
an orange twist.

FREUDIAN SLIP
Small wine glass

INGREDIENTS
**½ oz. anise liqueur
½ oz. Benedictine
½ oz. green apple liqueur
½ oz. lemon juice
½ oz. unfiltered apple juice
apple sherbet to garnish**

METHOD
Shake all ingredients with ice and
pour into apple sherbet—crusted
small wine glass.

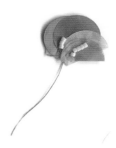

HEAVENLY HIBISCUS
Highball glass

INGREDIENTS

1½ oz. cognac
½ oz. vanilla liqueur
½ oz. hibiscus cordial
½ oz. lemon juice
2 oz. apple juice
dash of sugar syrup
wedge of green apple to garnish

METHOD

Shake all ingredients and serve
long into a chilled highball glass.
Garnish with a speared apple wedge.

BETWEEN THE SHEETS
Tumbler

INGREDIENTS

1 oz. brandy
½ oz. light rum
½ oz. triple sec
splash of sweet and sour mix

METHOD

Pour brandy, rum and triple sec into
an ice-filled tumbler. Fill with sweet
and sour mix and serve.

rock around the clock

❣

Rock 'n' roll and fashion have always shaken hands, done deals and helped each other along the way. That's why I've dedicated a chapter to them—my strongest loves of all. This cavalcade of drinks has been especially created for this book to suit your drinking and listening moods.

Where rock'n'roll brings out the inner wild child in us all, fashion helps us keep it neatly stitched together. After all, what does it matter if you're dancing wildly to a Motörhead song in a gorgeous Prada knit, killer heels and a $400 skirt with vintage clutch bag?

Bad boys like Bon Scott, Mick Jagger and Jimi Hendrix showed us their outlaw ways as rock icons, and they also showed us that there are two kinds of men in the world—those who stick around and those who don't. Unfortunately, they belonged to the latter. If you find yourself hanging on to these blokes, then at the very least, drink to their honor but don't succumb to their spell.

While you're toasting, raise a glass to couture and Hollywood glamour. For that starlet fever, look no further than the va-va-voom of Marilyn Monroe and Coco Chanel. Choose an icon, down a cocktail and be transformed for a night!

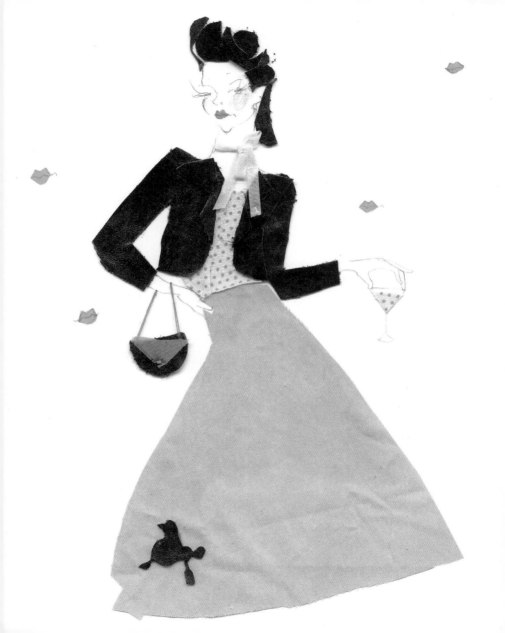

COCO CHANEL
Martini glass

INGREDIENTS
½ oz. white chocolate sauce
½ oz. crème de cacao
½ oz. ginger liqueur
½ oz. cognac
½ oz. heavy cream
½ oz. milk
white chocolate powder to garnish

METHOD
Shake all ingredients and pour into
a martini glass dusted with white
chocolate powder.

*Coco Chanel embodied style; she showed us the
purpose of that little black dress in the back of our
wardrobes. So pull out your best black number and
drink to the French queen of style and sophistication.*

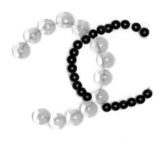

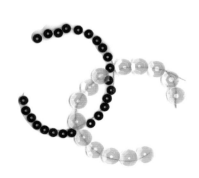

NICO

Martini glass

INGREDIENTS

1 oz. peach schnapps
1 oz. Tuaca
1 oz. pineapple juice
½ oz. guava juice
dash of grenadine and fruit-tea flakes
** to garnish**

METHOD

Shake all ingredients vigorously.
Strain into a chilled martini glass.
(It should have a thick foamy surface.)
To garnish, sprinkle a tiny amount of
grenadine to form an abstract pattern
on top and spoon a few fruit-tea flakes
in the center. (The garnish is only
effective if the tea and grenadine sit
firmly on the surface.)

*Nico became one of the most intriguing fringe
figures of the rock scene in the late 60s.
She was a diva who rose to fame as a European
supermodel and also performed in Fellini's*
La Dolce Vita *and started to hang out with
the Velvet Underground. This collaboration
came about thanks to pop artist Andy Warhol,
who encouraged her to be an occasional singer
with the band.*

MARILYN MONROE
Martini glass

INGREDIENTS
½ oz. honey dew liqueur
½ oz. Malibu
½ oz. cognac
I oz. lemon juice
2 tsp. sugar syrup
2 tsp. black raspberry liqueur
apple to garnish

METHOD
Pour all ingredients into a martini glass, stir, and garnish with skewered apple.

She once said, "Sex is part of nature. I go along with nature." Marilyn Monroe personified Hollywood glamour; she was a 50s sex goddess, a movie star who was much adored. She was synonymous with beauty, style and grace, and died at the age of 36. Her grandiosity lives on; drink this in honor of her.

MAE WEST
Highball glass

INGREDIENTS
I oz. rum
½ oz. amaretto
½ oz. blackberry liqueur
I½ oz. pineapple juice
2 cherries to garnish

METHOD
Shake and strain all ingredients into a highball glass. Garnish with 2 cherries on a toothpick.

Mae West was a Hollywood sex symbol for 50 years and earned her stripes working as an actor on Broadway. She was born in Brooklyn in 1893 and became known for that sultry voice, perfect hourglass figure and irreverent style. She died in LA in 1980.

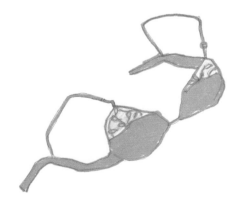

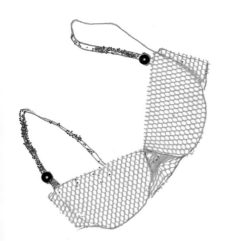

DOLLY PARTON
Tumbler

INGREDIENTS
1 oz. Absolut Mandarin
½ oz. Southern Comfort
½ oz. butterscotch schnapps
½ oz. lemon juice
2 oz. white cranberry juice

METHOD
Shake and strain all ingredients
into a tumbler.

For a bosom full of love, look no further than
the peroxide-blond goddess of country music
—Dolly Parton. She's one part Barbie, two parts
woman. So when you've stopped working nine
to five, down this for refreshment.

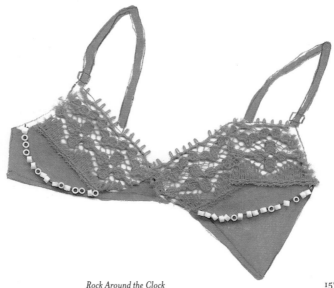

JOAN JETT
Highball glass

INGREDIENTS
3 wedges of lime
2 oz. rum
splash of cola

METHOD
Squeeze lime wedges into a highball
glass, discarding the pieces. Build rum
and cola over ice.

Joan Jett's signature anthem, "I Love Rock 'n' Roll,"
was belted out wearing a fitted black leather waist
jacket. She was an outlaw; she was sexy and she
rocked—first with her band The Runaways in the
70s and then with the Blackhearts in the 80s. This
drink is for rockers and rollers, pure and simple.

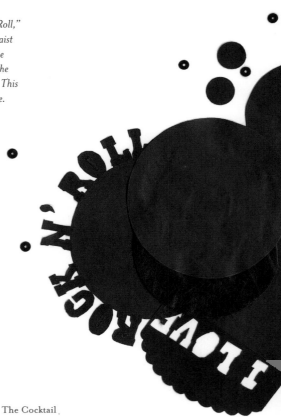

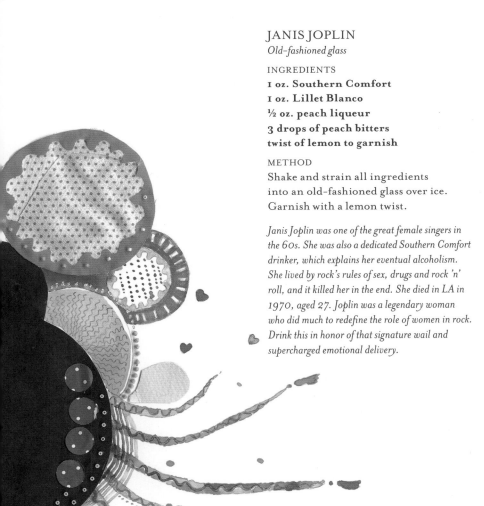

JANIS JOPLIN
Old-fashioned glass

INGREDIENTS
1 oz. Southern Comfort
1 oz. Lillet Blanco
½ oz. peach liqueur
3 drops of peach bitters
twist of lemon to garnish

METHOD
Shake and strain all ingredients
into an old-fashioned glass over ice.
Garnish with a lemon twist.

Janis Joplin was one of the great female singers in the 60s. She was also a dedicated Southern Comfort drinker, which explains her eventual alcoholism. She lived by rock's rules of sex, drugs and rock 'n' roll, and it killed her in the end. She died in LA in 1970, aged 27. Joplin was a legendary woman who did much to redefine the role of women in rock. Drink this in honor of that signature wail and supercharged emotional delivery.

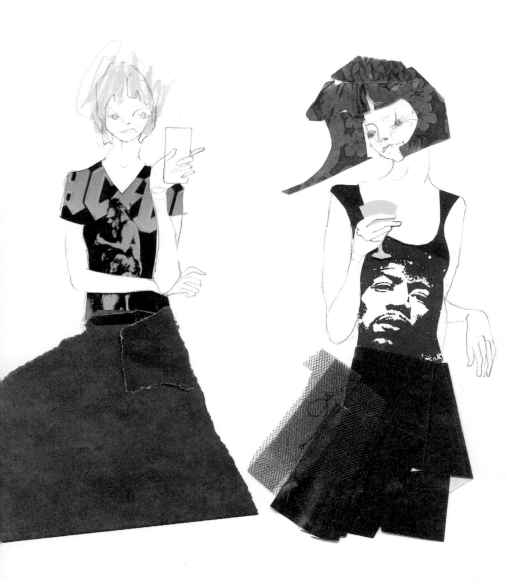

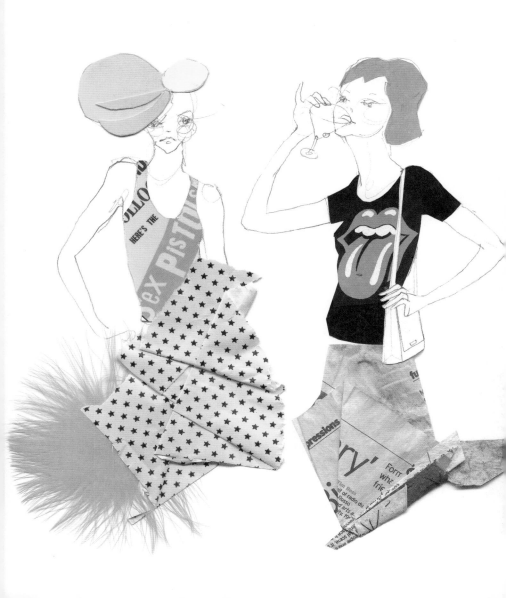

BON SCOTT
Highball glass

INGREDIENTS
1 fig
½ lime
1 tsp. brown sugar
2 oz. rum
splash of ginger ale
slice of fig to garnish

METHOD
Muddle fig, lime and sugar, then churn
with crushed ice and rum. Pour into
a highball glass. Top with ginger ale.
Garnish with a slice of fig.

Bon Scott personified everything that was sexily
rebellious. It didn't get more primal or sexually
motivated than Scott, who joined AC/DC as a
front man for five years. He was a legend, breaking
many hearts as he shagged his way around town.
His most famous quote: "It keeps you fit—the alcohol,
nasty women, sweat on stage, bad food—it's all
very good for you." He died in 1980, aged 33.

GINNY HENDRIX
Martini glass

INGREDIENTS
4 wedges of lime
1 tsp. superfine sugar
2 oz. gin
½ oz. white crème de cacao
chocolate powder to garnish

METHOD
Muddle lime and sugar. Add gin,
crème de cacao and crushed ice to fill.
Serve in a martini glass dusted with
chocolate powder.

Jimi Hendrix redefined cool in the late 60s with his
unique self-taught guitar-playing ways. He was
a shy fellow but a sexy one. He oozed charm and
charisma and put a new spin on rock fashion. His
appeal was embodied in the sexy sounds he created
through sweaty rock, funk and soul. Long live the
master who told us, "The story of life is quicker than
the blink of an eye, the story of love is hello, goodbye."

SID VICIOUS
Martini glass

INGREDIENTS
2 ½ oz. vodka
I tsp. sauvignon blanc
I passionfruit
maraschino cherry to garnish

METHOD
Fill glass with ice. In a shaker, combine ice, vodka and wine, and double-strain into a martini glass. Drizzle passionfruit pulp into glass and garnish with a safety-pin-skewered cherry.

Oh, what a figure of British punk rock we have here. It was all about anarchy and nihilism for this little punk rock boy who believed in taking everything to extremes. He was a rebel with a cause, but his junkie lifestyle couldn't hold him together for very long. Sid Vicious embodied everything that was disaffected and angst-driven in London in the 70s. We've all dated a guy like this—the one who isn't worth chasing any longer, but was definitely fun to chase in the beginning.

MICK JAGGARD
Martini glass

INGREDIENTS
2 squeezes of lime
I ½ oz. Jaggard original
½ oz. Cointreau
I ½ oz. cranberry juice
twist of lime to garnish

METHOD
Shake and strain all ingredients into a martini glass. Garnish with a lime twist.

Mick Jagger once said, "It's all right letting yourself go, as long as you can get yourself back." That he has well and truly done, from mad drug days in the late 60s to rocking the panties off many a woman, even at age 60. He's dated the finest, from Marianne Faithfull to Jerry Hall. Drink this in celebration of the man who gave this quote: "Anything worth doing is worth overdoing."

ACKNOWLEDGMENTS

I want to thank Kirsten Abbott for approaching me with the idea for this book and for making it happen. Thanks to Emma Schwarcz at Hardie Grant, who took on the project midway and encouraged me wholeheartedly, and especially for being so damn fussy to make sure all measurements were completely accurate!

Thanks to my partner Billy Walsh and the Cherry Bar entourage (you know who you are, you maniacs who don't believe in measuring ingredients! Osker and Nat especially, you crazy cats).

To my friends Helen Razer and Susan King and to my dear friend Monica Levy, who helped me with all those gorgeous Sydney bars and hunted down the best bartenders for unique recipes—the tequila chapter is dedicated to you, babe!

To my mum and dad, need I say more, your support is endless.

To my editors at *The Age*, *Sydney Sun Herald*, *West Australian* and *NW* (Tiffany Dunk), who have supported me throughout my writing career.

Other very special thanks go to the legendary talents of bartenders who supplied such gorgeous recipes for this book: Grant Collins from the Water Bar, W Hotel; Mark Ward from Hugo's Group, founder of Yakusan; Mike Enright from The Loft Sydney; Matthew Bax from Der Raum Melbourne; Simon Page from Transport Public Bar; Cleo Seaman from The Como Hotel; Daniel Rosette from Terra Firma Northcote; Marcus Motteram from ffour; Murray Pitman from The Gin Palace; Tony Starr's Kitten Club; Phoenix; Misty Bar; Hairy Canary; and Café Pacifico Sydney.

Other inspiration comes from music, from the Supersuckers to Motörhead —do yourself a favor and find yourself some decent music to get wasted to!

INDEX

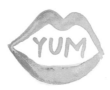